Praise for Bob Doyle's *Follow Your Passion, Find Your Power*

"Outstanding! Finally, a clear guide to making your life work!"

—Dr. Joe Vitale, author of *The Attractor Factor*

"Bob was teaching the principles of the Law of Attraction LONG before it emerged as cultural jargon. In this book, Bob takes the mystery right out, offering plain speak on how you can truly apply the principles so they work. More importantly, he offers strategies for releasing and clearing, an essential piece missing from most instruction. If you are ready for a life that has more grace, ease, and peace in it, then get this book right now."

—Jennifer McLean, author, speaker,
creator of Body Dialoging,
and host of "Healing with the Masters"

"Love it! *Follow Your Passion, Find Your Power* is one of the most important, unique, and brilliant books you'll ever read on the Law of Attraction. Bob Doyle reveals what it *really* takes to make this universal law work in your life. Read it cover to cover. Then, read it again."

—Sonia Ricotti, bestselling author of
The Law of Attraction, Plain and Simple
and *Unsinkable*

"In *Follow Your Passion, Find Your Power*, Bob has beautifully created a life approach that distills abstract principles into simple and very powerful tools. Best of all, through his personal sharing, readers will instantly see themselves, be able to draw parallels, and more quickly learn from one of the most authentic and astute teachers in the field of deliberate living. This book is all most readers will need to jumpstart their life into high gear."

—Mike Dooley, *New York Times*
bestselling author of *Infinite Possibilities*

"In *Follow your Passion, Find your Power*, Bob Doyle reveals the larger secret of the Law of Attraction. Find the truth of your soul's desire to contribute to the world, and you find your passion. And above all, the universe rewards passion."

—James Redfield, author of
The Celestine Prophecy and
The Twelfth Insight

FOLLOW YOUR PASSION, FIND YOUR POWER

Everything You Need to Know About the Law of Attraction

BOB DOYLE

Foreword by Marci Shimoff

With contributions by:
Janet Bray Attwood, Hale Dwoskin & Carol Look

This edition first published in 2011 by
Hampton Roads Publishing Company, Inc.
Charlottesville, VA 22906
www.hrpub.com

Originally published in 2003 by Boundless Living Publishing / Trafford Publishing. ISBN: 978-1412013604

ISBN: 978-1-57174-647-4
Library of Congress Cataloging-in-Publication Data is available upon request.

Cover design by Jim Warner
Cover image © Ikon Images / SuperStock
Author photo by Bob Doyle

Printed in the United States of America
TS
10 9 8 7 6 5 4 3 2 1

Printed on 30% post-consumer waste recycled paper.

Contents

Foreword by Marci Shimoff

It's been great to see in recent years that the Law of Attraction has become the subject of a worldwide conversation. Yet, even with all of the talk about it, I've noticed that many people are still not getting the results they want. So it's the perfect time for a book like this that deepens and clarifies people's understanding of this fundamental key to a more fulfilling life.

When, a few years ago, I was invited to appear in the film *The Secret,* it was the manifestation of one of my dreams. It was deeply rewarding for me to have the opportunity to share a body of knowledge I was passionate about with what turned out to be a global audience. And one of the many benefits that experience has brought to my life has been getting to know the other teachers in the film, whom I admire and respect. Among my favorites is Bob Doyle.

Many people do a good job of teaching the principles of the Law of Attraction. But only a few live those principles and are able to teach this deep wisdom both in words and by example. That's Bob, 100 percent. Bob and I first met when we were keynote speakers at the W8 Global Conference in Manzanillo, Mexico. My topic was "Happiness and the Law of Attraction"; Bob's was "Wealth Beyond Reason."

From the first moment I met him, I knew Bob was the real deal. There's no hype about Bob—you talk with him and you know he's a solid guy. I found him to be warm, loving, and supportive of me and my work. And I was deeply impressed with his ability to tell the *whole* story of the Law of Attraction in completely accessible, easy, and practical terms.

Bob's been a great colleague ever since. We've shared on teleseminars, interviews, and at speeches a number of times, and every time I hear Bob speak, I appreciate his mainstream approach to the Law of Attraction. He keeps it very real and down-to-earth and at the same time reveals an exceptionally deep and thorough understanding of the Law.

I really listen to whatever Bob says. I know I can trust him to speak the truth from his own direct experience of it. So I'm very happy to see that, in this book, Bob is clarifying points about the Law of Attraction and clearing up some common misunderstandings. In my travels around the world in the years following the tremendous popularity of *The Secret*, I've seen firsthand the success and fulfillment many have enjoyed as a result of understanding these principles. But I have also seen the frustration of others who were less successful because of misconceptions and myths they heard about the Law of Attraction.

In *Follow Your Passion*, Bob makes it clear that the Law is not a personal development tool you can use the right way or wrong way; it's a profound statement of how Energy works in the Universe. He explains the critical role that our belief systems play, and shows how to dissolve the resistances that arise from limiting belief systems. Further, he helps you clarify your vision into one that inspires you and aligns you with the creative Energy of the Universe.

Bob also addresses the importance of tapping into the power of your passions. If you are living your passion with limited resistance, then you will be able to use the Law of Attraction to your best advantage— and it will help you manifest your dreams and live a life of true wealth.

Another key to success with the Law of Attraction that you will learn in this book is how to listen to your intuition. Bob teaches you how to hear what your intuition is telling you and then let it lead you into inspired action.

These are principles I've used over the course of my life. I believe in them because they've worked so well for me. Whenever I move beyond my limiting beliefs, listen to my intuition, and follow my passions, my life unfolds in magical ways.

I'm particularly delighted that Bob truly understands the correlation between happiness and the Law of Attraction. As we in the personal development industry often say: Success doesn't bring happiness; happiness bring success. When you align with your passion, you experience greater happiness and invite more success into your life.

Take this journey with Bob. You are going to love the ride and the true wealth you'll experience in your life as a result. Understanding the immutable Law of Attraction provides a key to your success—but you have to use the key properly. This book lights the way.

Introduction

In May of 2005, I was sitting in a hotel room in Austin, Texas when I received a phone call from a woman identifying herself as Rhonda Byrne, an Australian television producer. She informed me that she was working on a film project based on the Law of Attraction.

I had been teaching the Law of Attraction through my online program, Wealth Beyond Reason, for about three years and had established something of a reputation for teaching these principles in a mainstream, down-to-earth way. Ms. Byrne told me that she had been very impressed with the way my program taught the principles of the Law of Attraction, and that she'd like for me to be a part of her movie project, which she was calling *The Secret*.

By this time, I'd been approached by a handful of people who wanted me to participate in their ambitious film or television projects. Quite honestly, I had become a bit jaded; virtually none of these projects ever got off the ground. So while I was polite and listened to Ms. Byrne's pitch, I was a bit dubious that this project would actually ever see the light of day.

That is, of course, until she suggested that I go online and take a look at the conceptual "trailer" she had put together for the film. I told her I'd be happy to take a look at it.

In my mind I was expecting the kind of slide presentation I'd seen many times before. But what I saw was a full-blown, Hollywood-quality movie trailer, complete with a powerful musical score and top-notch production.

This woman was for real . . . and I wanted in.

Fast forward two years. *The Secret* had spread first across the Internet, then on DVD and in book form, like absolute wildfire. Featured not once but twice on the *Oprah Winfrey Show, The Secret* was the talk of the town all over the world, and the Law of Attraction was the hottest ticket in the personal development industry.

While this was good on many levels, it had its downsides. Many people jumped on the Law of Attraction bandwagon, classifying themselves as experts and creating products and programs based on the most basic Law of Attraction principles. Catch phrases such as "like attracts like" and "what you focus on expands" became the popular definitions of the Law of Attraction—and while these statements are ways in which the Law of Attraction can occur, they only tell a small part of the story. This misunderstanding of the concepts of the Law of Attraction ultimately led many to frustration and disappointment."

While *The Secret* was mostly met with enthusiasm in the "self help" circles, the mainstream was not so quick to embrace the principles put forth in the film. In part, this was because the film was only about ninety minutes, and certainly couldn't flesh out all of the critical concepts related to such a complex concept. So while some people were able to have powerful "ah-ha" moments after watching *The Secret* and make quick and powerful changes in their lives, others met with lackluster results at best, and others outright rejected the idea that we could "create our lives by design."

It wasn't long before the honeymoon was over, and I found myself creating more content addressing the misconceptions related to what was taught in *The Secret* than new content for my students. However, I think this is a good thing. It's not at all surprising that ideas like those being put forth in the film would be met with rejection by many. After all, the majority of people do not experience "doing, being, and having" anything they desire; in fact, for many the reality is the complete opposite.

But there is a reason for that—a sound, scientific reason to which the Law of Attraction holds the explanation. It is ironic that the Law of Attraction can clearly explain why an individual has all the proof they need in their lives to disprove the Law of Attraction!

It has been six years since my first book, *Wealth Beyond Reason,* was published, and that was three years before *The Secret* was created. Because *The Secret* was such a phenomenon, and because there was such a subsequent glut of Law of Attraction material thrown into the marketplace—much of which only told a small part of the story, and was thus largely ineffective at changing people's lives in a significant way—the Law of Attraction is something about which people are simply tired of hearing.

They may have tried various programs without results. In some cases, they may have found their situations getting worse than they were when they started. Again, there is a reason this happens, but if you don't have all the information, the whole thing simply becomes confusing and frustrating. It's no wonder that people give up on the Law of Attraction, or decide that it's not real.

One of the goals of this book is to address head-on the objections, questions, and comments that have surfaced since the release of *The Secret.* I didn't write this book to defend the film or the Law of Attraction, neither of which need defending. Instead, this book is meant to address the completely legitimate questions that naturally arise for people when such a new and radical concept enters their brain space!

I'm passionate about teaching the truth about the Law of Attraction because it changed my life dramatically, and I've seen it do the same for countless others over the years. It is my desire to see human beings live lives of pure passion, abundance, and prosperity, and I believe that a complete understanding of the Law of Attraction can facilitate that for those who are struggling. Is it absolutely necessary to understand the Law of Attraction to live a fulfilling life? Absolutely not. Many people live amazing lives without any knowledge of the energetic nature of the Universe, the power of their thoughts, or the Law of Attraction. And yes, there's a reason why that is true as well.

This book will provide answers to common questions about the Law of Attraction and living your life by design. I will not use "woo woo" terminology or New Age speak. My hope is that anyone of any background will be able to understand the truth of these principles clearly after reading this book—and more importantly, that they will be able to implement what they've learned and begin taking inspired action toward the life of their dreams.

And yes, action is involved. We are each engaged in an energetic dance with the rest of the Universe of which we are a part. The Law of Attraction is always at work, and we are always interacting with the rest of the Universe on an energetic level. Every thought we have has an impact. It is the action we take, however, that puts things into motion. Let the action of reading this book be the first step towards a true understanding of the miracle that is the human experience. Begin to powerfully create the masterpiece your life is to become!

Chapter 1

INTRODUCTION TO THE LAW OF ATTRACTION AND RESISTANCE

How the Law of Attraction Came Into My Life

I want to clarify right away that I'm not a physicist or any other kind of formally trained scientist. Nor does one need to be to utilize Law of Attraction principles. While I ground virtually everything I teach in science, I do not play the role of a quantum physicist because I have found that for the most part, people's eyes begin to glaze over when my explanations of the

Law of Attraction become too complicated. After all, if you felt you needed a mathematics degree to be able to create your life by design, the entire process would be too daunting to take on in the first place.

A basic understanding of the physics of the Law of Attraction is essential to fully integrating many of the ideas discussed in this book. I believe you'll find most of the ideas to be utterly fascinating rather than overwhelming, and my hope is that you will find this part of the education to be as fun and inspiring as I do.

When I began investigating the whole idea of "creating reality" (as I called it when I first began exploring the concept in the early 1990s), I was absolutely turned on by the idea that we have more control over our experience of reality than we as humans are generally aware of.

I will never forget the fateful evening of December 26, 1990 when a friend of mine and I were marveling over the technical wonders of a special "holographic" paper wrapped around a pencil we picked up at a convenience store. Depending on how light hit it, a truly unbelievable array of colors would shoot forth from the paper in three dimensions. It looked as if it were lit electronically somehow from the inside. I remember truly marveling that science had created such an amazing light show that only a decade before would have cost literally thousands of dollars to create, and yet now was available for pennies on stickers, notebooks, and countless other trinkets one could pick up at any gas station.

It was while I was in this mindset of "anything is possible" that I received what I can only call a "download" from the Universe, an ah-ha moment to beat all ah-ha moments: Everything Is Energy.

Again, I've never received any kind of formal scientific training aside from what I learned in high school. But what I received in that moment was a knowing. I could clearly see the energetic nature of the Universe and how everything in the Universe is connected and has influence over everything else—even if we can't detect it with the five senses we've been trained to acknowledge.

I was so affected by the information that came to me at that moment that I spent the next twelve years of my life trying to make enough sense of it to actually do something with it. In that time I read several books, but most of my work was inner work. I learned to meditate. I studied hypnosis. I became totally fascinated with quantum physics, Energy, and the power of the mind.

With all that study came a strong intellectual understanding that actually creating life by design was all somehow truly possible, and that people were doing it. However, a very big piece of the puzzle was still missing for me. Although I read several books that were scientific in nature, there were some dots that weren't connecting for me. I realized that although understanding on a conscious and intellectual level that "anything is possible" was a good start, there was another level of understanding and believing that I was going to need in order fully integrate the idea that I could consciously create my reality into my worldview.

My breakthrough finally came in October of 2002. I had quit my corporate job in January of that year because it was literally killing me to go there day after day and feel absolutely no sense of myself or my value in what I was doing. And although the money was good, I had still managed to accumulate roughly sixty thousand dollars in debt. No matter how many raises I got (and I was making just under one hundred thousand dollars a year when I quit), my financial situation continued to decline.

More important than my financial situation was this feeling that my life was literally being drained from me. Like most people, I wanted to have a career that I was passionate about and in which I could express myself fully and creatively. Sitting in a windowless office working on human resources software did not afford me that opportunity, and finally the day came that in spite of my personal economic crisis, I simply *had* to walk away from being an employee.

My plan was to fully involve myself in teaching people to create their realities using all the information I'd been researching for over a decade. The only problem was that I wasn't an actual living example of what I was teaching. Still, I forged ahead. I created audio programs on the subject, and tried (mostly in vain) to book myself at hotels to speak and sell CDs and tapes—because that's what I believe I had to do to be a part of the self-help industry.

I studied marketing like my life depended on it (which I believed it did), and tried so hard to make sales and convince people that I knew what I was talking about. At that point, I didn't feel out of integrity because I truly believed everything I was teaching. But the truth was that there was something I wasn't getting.

No matter how hard I worked, no matter how much new information about marketing I learned, and no matter how good my intentions were, nothing was changing for me—except that my money problems continued to increase.

My wife and I reached a breaking point when our financial woes forced her to return to work. This was a major blow to my ego, as it had taken me many years to convince her to quit the job that was making her so miserable. After all, my corporate job was paying well enough (I was great at ignoring the truth about our financial situation), and my wife finally resigned from her position so she could stay home with our young children and be a full-time mother.

Because I'd made such a big deal about how we could afford for her to quit her job, my wife's return to work was a major wake-up call for me. I suddenly became clear that all this "work" I was doing wasn't getting me anywhere. All this trying to "figure out what was wrong" wasn't producing any answers. I finally decided to step back and become a true student of my own teaching.

That meant giving the whole thing up to a much more intelligent power.

Much of what I'd learned was that if you were clear about your vision and held it, the Universe would provide you with the answers and resources you needed to move forward. Those answers came in the form of something called intuition. For the nine months after I left my job, the voice of my intuition was being drowned out by the screaming of my ego and intellect, and it was time to quiet the noise and listen to what was being sent to me.

My new strategy became simply to get very clear on what I wanted (a career I was passionate about); being aware of what was showing up in my life; and taking definitive action at every step, regardless of whether it made logical sense or not. Truth be told, that is absolutely all you need to know about making the Law of Attraction work in your life. What makes it more difficult than it seems is the Energy that's running deep within us that we don't even know about. Learning about that Energy was the key to my eventual success.

To summarize what happened to me over the coming weeks, I'll simply say that I began to pay attention to things that I might have overlooked as trivial or irrelevant to my goals in the past. Conversations with new people gave rise to opportunities to explore various resources that I would never have found if I'd kept looking to my intellect for all the answers. A series of chance meetings eventually led me to discover a book called *A Happy Pocket Full of Money* by David Cameron Gikandi.

This book is what finally turned on the lights for me by clarifying in new ways several of the principles I'd already learned. The most important distinction

I learned was just how powerful my belief system was, specifically my limiting beliefs about money and success. Gikandi's book explains the physics of our thoughts in such a way that I finally understood that thoughts are not just dormant ideas floating around somewhere in our brain, but that—like everything else in the Universe—they are real Energy, and thus have a real effect on my own experience of reality!

What were my limiting beliefs? Growing up in a single-parent home, the son of a school teacher who did not like her job, my family constantly experienced a lack of money. I learned that money was hard to come by, debt was always present, and in the end, it didn't matter whether you enjoyed what you did to earn money or not. You simply had to do what it took to bring in money.

When I could clearly see that these beliefs had run over the course of my life, it was easy for me to understand why all my attempts at generating revenue through businesses of my own, or through other means, always resulted in disappointment. My belief system simply didn't support my having financial success!

This revelation was a huge breakthrough for me. In that moment, I realized that my number one priority was to go to work on my beliefs, and that instead of filling my head and emotional state with fear and worry about money, I needed to find ways to saturate myself in feelings of abundance to the best of my ability. I understood at that time that it didn't matter how much I consciously *desired* a different situation; if my belief system wasn't congruent with that success, it simply was impossible for me to experience it. You'll learn more specifically why that is as we explore the concept of *resistance* and how the Law of Attraction really works.

If you watched *The Secret,* you learned about Vision Boards. These can take many forms, but essentially they are something of a visual collage of the things that you want to attract into your life. I'll share more details on vision boards as well as other techniques later, but this is a technique I began using right away. Because I spend so much time at my computer, I decided to use my computer's background wallpaper as my vision board. I began by taking a screenshot of my online banking statement. Then, in an image editing program, I changed all the numbers (which were pathetically low at the time) to very large numbers, unlike any I'd ever seen in my bank account. At first, of course, these numbers seemed unrealistic and way too huge to ever come true.

However, after days of looking at these new numbers, I stopped reacting in such a dubious way. The numbers became the norm in my mind.

What I had done was stretch my energetic comfort zone around my bank account. As you'll learn, this is essential if you wish to significantly change your financial situation for the better.

So did money just magically appear in my bank account because I did this exercise? Of course not. What did happen was that I was provided with more and more creative inspiration about actions to take that would result in generating money. By now I'd learned not to judge these ideas, but to immediately move into what I was inspired to do. In my case, the inspiration was to put together an online program where I would share what I was learning. I called the program Wealth Beyond Reason, and its creation marked the beginning of a whole new life for me.

Another thing I did was absolutely key. It's something I'll be reiterating often. Rather than enter the online world of personal development with the mindset that "one day I'll be successful at this" or "eventually I'll be as effective as so-and-so who's already doing it," I made a commitment to myself to step powerfully into already *being* who I aspired to be. There is a huge difference from an energetic point of view (what you're "putting out there") between "wanting" to be something and "already being it."

I can't go too much further in my story without going into a more in-depth explanation of the energetic nature of this Universe we live in and providing what I believe to be the most accurate definition and explanation of how the Law of Attraction really works, so let's get into that right now.

The Truth about the Law of Attraction

Probably one of the biggest misconceptions about the Law of Attraction is that it's some kind of new personal development technique. Because of the success of *The Secret* and the subsequent influx of programs purporting to teach the Law of Attraction, many people started to view the Law of Attraction as some kind of "trick" or technique. This creates a mindset that the Law of Attraction can *work* or *not work* depending on whether or not one "does it right."

The whole notion that the Law of Attraction is something one "does" or "activates" is at the core of the misunderstanding that causes people to give up utilizing the principle to shape their lives.

Let's get this very clear: The Law of Attraction is *not* a tool or technique, and it is not all about "getting stuff." The Law of Attraction explains the behavior of Energy. It's a *much* bigger concept than simply how we as human beings can shape our experience of reality.

Remember, everything is Energy. This is something that science tells us for certain. Everything in our Universe, tangible or not, is composed of Energy in various forms, vibrating at various frequencies.

What we experience as physical reality, for example, is the result of our interpretation of Energy through our senses. As humans, we experience things as "physical" if they fall into a specific range of frequencies. At higher frequencies, things become less "visible" to us. Thoughts, for example, vibrate at a much higher frequency than does a chair; thoughts are not visible to the eye. Nonetheless, they obviously exist.

To use another example, there are colors in the spectrum of all possible colors that our eyes cannot see, but that *can* be seen by a snake. Dogs can hear frequencies of sound (also Energy) that we cannot hear. Those frequencies simply vibrate at a frequency that is out in our range.

As energetic beings, the Energy that makes up who we are is always vibrating at some frequency or series of frequencies. We call this our "vibration."

The most important concept that we need to understand as human beings attempting to work with these principles is something called *resonance.* If vibrational frequencies are in resonance, they attract. The opposite of resonance is *dissonance.* If vibrational frequencies are dissonant, they repel.

This is where I have a problem with the "like attracts like" definition of the Law of Attraction. While this can be the case sometimes, it is *not* the definition of the Law of Attraction, and certainly doesn't explain the behavior of Energy across the board. For example, many will be quick to point out that it is opposite polarities of a magnet that actually attract. And what about Mr. and Mrs. Jones who are clearly not at all alike, and yet are very much in love and most definitely attracted to each other?

You see, it's not about vibrational frequencies being the same. What determines whether the attraction process takes place is whether or not there is *resonance.*

You may have heard someone say that they resonate with a person, or an idea, or a piece of music. There is a vibrational harmony that takes place on an invisible level of Energy, and it results in an emotional state. For example, if you resonate with a piece of music, your emotional state will shift in some way that keeps you listening to it, wanting more, or simply enjoying it. This doesn't necessarily mean that the feelings you have are always positive. You may hear a sad piece of music and still resonate with it; your emotional state shifts accordingly.

Dissonance works differently. If you hear music that you absolutely can't listen to for whatever reason, it is because there is energetic dissonance. No attraction takes place, and in fact you experience a literal repulsion to the music.

Understanding resonance and dissonance is absolutely key to working intentionally with the Law of Attraction because you want to be absolutely sure that you are in vibrational resonance with what you're trying to attract. So although the scope of the Law of Attraction goes way beyond how it affects the human experience, the aspect of this law that we need to understand in terms of creating our lives by design is this:

We attract into our experience those things with which we are in vibrational resonance.

I've previously mentioned the fallacy that the Law of Attraction is something that you "activate" or "turn on." The Law of Attraction is always on, and is always responding to your energetic vibration, bringing you more of the things with which you are in vibrational resonance. It doesn't matter whether you're consciously trying to attract something or not. If you're in resonance with it, you are in the process of attracting it. Most people are attracting by default.

It's also important to fully understand the role of our emotions when working with the Law of Attraction. They are the very force that determines our vibration and tells us to a great extent what our vibrational state is in a given moment.

Law of Attraction teachers are often criticized by people who challenge the idea that we are attracting all parts of our experience by pointing to situations in the world where they claim that the person or people involved could not have possibly attracted said situation. Natural disasters, terrorist attacks, birth defects, and the like are all pointed at as evidence that we do not attract everything into our experience and that some things just happen without explanation.

This criticism comes from the false notion that proponents of Law of Attraction suggest that everything about the attraction process is based in consciousness; that in order for something to happen to someone, they must have consciously invited it on some level. Perhaps some Law of Attraction teachers are saying that, but I definitely do not subscribe to that line of thinking. Again, the Law of Attraction is not simply some kind of "tool" that allows humans to manifest things or create their lives. It's much, much bigger than that.

If something happens to someone, it does not mean they necessarily wanted it to happen. It doesn't mean they visualized it, created a vision board, or meditated it into reality. It simply means that for whatever reason, they were in vibrational resonance with it. The truth is that there are situations in which we can never know from the outside looking in how a person happened to get into resonance with an event that we deem bad, negative, or tragic. Sometimes we might be able to get some idea or create a theory, but the truth is that our own personal energetic vibrations are extremely complex—the result of a lifetime of experiences from the circumstances in our homes and schools, interaction with friends, what we see on television, read in books, and so on. Every single experience we have in our lives on both conscious and subconscious levels goes into our energetic construct, and every little nuance of that Energy creates our vibration.

With that level of vibrational complexity, it would be virtually impossible for anyone to look at a situation and know for certain how a person attracted it if it is not clearly evident.

Another more philosophical question is this: Whose experience is it anyway? If you look at a tragedy and have a reaction to it, what's really happening there? You are having the experience of watching another person or set of people have an experience. At a more quantum level, the Energy that composes the person that is you and your sensory system is interpreting another cluster of Energy in such a way that you create in your own mind the experience of "someone else" having an experience that you are interpreting as tragic. All you can really say for absolute certain is that you are having an experience that you are interpreting as someone else having an experience. Mind-boggling perhaps, but still true.

Obviously, most experiences you have in your waking life *seem* like reality. Again, this is how we've been taught to think, and it's a belief system that works for us as humans. The point is that when you realize that every single emotional experience you have is the result of an interpretation that you have *learned* how to make, then you can begin to accept the fact that you have a choice in how you interpret *any* situation, even though it may seem completely unnatural to do so given how you've been taught to respond in various circumstances.

We need only to look at religion to see how humanity can be divided on ideas about what is good or bad, true or false, good and evil. Within each religion, you have people who know only their own version of truth and reject all others. Does this make them right or wrong? The fact is that what they attract will depend on what is *truly* going on with their belief systems at an energetic level (that is, what they truly believe at their core as compared to what they may dogmatically *say* they believe).

This is to say that spending a great deal of time trying to interpret the truth of a situation that is not our own is very often an act of futility and a misuse of our own Energy. Ultimately, our experience of life as a whole will be dependent on our own vibration and what we allow into our "space."

Therefore, what we really need to understand is how we as human beings can shift our vibration so that we are in resonance with what we want. That way we can literally attract it, rather than putting our emotion and attention into things we do not like or want to be part of our experience. Further, we need to understand what Energy systems might be running within us that are actually repelling what we want; we must learn to eliminate those patterns to allow what we want to flow freely to us in the most efficient way possible. We'll soon talk about the various ways that the Universe responds to our vibrational "requests" and how to actually make those requests, but it's first absolutely essential to understand more about the force that will slow or stop the attraction process. That force is referred to as resistance.

Resistance

If there was something that the movie *The Secret* could probably have been addressed more, it's the topic of *resistance*. Without an understanding of what resistance is and how to deal with it, your work with the Law of Attraction will be hit-and-miss at best.

Resistance explains why some people can take the exact same action as other people and not have similar results. Resistance explains why no matter how long you meditate, visualize, work on your vision boards, or engage in any other Law of Attraction technique, you still aren't getting the results you desire—many times you're getting the complete opposite results.

In the last chapter, I discussed resonance and dissonance. Dissonance is what happens as the result of resistance. Within the scope of the Law of Attraction conversation, resistance can be defined as "any system of Energy that is *not* in resonance with what you're trying to attract." Resistance lives largely in our belief system.

For example, if your desire is great financial wealth, but your belief system includes ideas such as "money is too hard to come by," "money is bad," or "if I get money, I'll just lose it and things will be even worse," then these thoughts are emitting a vibrational frequency that is absolutely not in resonance with the idea "I enjoy having a lot of money!" Therefore, the attraction process simply cannot take place. It's a scientific impossibility.

Does that mean you won't acquire a lot of money? No. In fact, in my situation I was making what many would call a great living in the corporate world. A six-figure salary is the dream of countless people. I had that, and yet I had no money. Why? Because my belief system about money was that there was never enough, and that there would always be debt. As a result, my life was in alignment with that Energy.

You've probably heard of people winning huge amounts of money in the lottery, only to lose it within a few short years or months. While they were able to get into resonance with winning that amount of money, their energetic wealth "set point" was way below what they received. The resistance that resulted literally forced the money out of their lives through events that took place, or actions taken by the winner that were more congruent with their true beliefs about money.

Have you ever come extremely close to realizing a dream only to have something happen to bring you back to square one? Do you recognize a pattern of self-sabotage in your life in those areas that are most important to you in terms of goals?

Any time you see a pattern, this is a strong signal that you have an energetic program running. You are literally programmed to either behave in a certain way at some point in your progress, or attract certain circumstances that will hinder that progress. This is because of the energetic patterns that are set in place. Because the Universe is always responding to every vibration you emit, it is your predominant vibration that you are going to experience the most of. If you hold a deeply rooted belief system that you cannot really have what you want, you are literally in resonance with the failure to reach your goal because your belief system is more in alignment with failure than with success.

Where did this resistance originate? Virtually everyone has some level of resistance, accumulated over many years of life from a variety of influences. Most obviously, we tend to take on large portions of the belief systems harbored by our parents. Our young minds take in what is demonstrated to us as absolute truth because we have nothing else to compare it with. If our parents say and demonstrate that money is hard to come by, which was my case, then we tend to integrate those beliefs to the extent that we see absolutely no other option. Even when we are adults and can look out into the world and see evidence that is contrary to our belief system, we often find it impossible to change the core beliefs that were implanted in us in our formative years.

It's not just parents who pass on these belief systems. We are also heavily influenced by our teachers, governments, clergy, and society as a whole.

The fact is that there is no universal truth that money is hard to come by, or that all men are jerks, or that you were "dealt a bad hand." However, a strong belief in those things will create an emotional state inside you that will generate a vibrational frequency that is in alignment with circumstances that are in vibrational alignment with those beliefs. Thus, you'll have all the evidence that you need to "prove" your belief system is true.

However, there are plenty of people who do *not* share those beliefs. Their emotional states around these issues are completely different, and so they attract circumstances that perpetuate their own belief systems.

Everyone gets to be "right" about their beliefs. The wonderful truth is that you get to choose your beliefs, and can therefore change the evidence that comes your way!

But resistance often runs very deep. After all, if you're an adult, you've lived a considerable numbers of years running these Energy systems—and they're fairly powerful programs. It will take more than just an intellectual understanding that you can change your belief system and a desire to do so to rewrite that program. Still, the true desire to change your belief system is an essential first step.

We know that very often there is a great deal of resistance to changing lifelong belief systems, even when we know they're not serving us. It's important to delve deep into the root beliefs that cause these belief systems to persist. Many people will insist that they want to acquire great wealth, because consciously they understand that having plenty of money will make their lives easier in many ways. But what if on a deeper level they have a belief that money is bad, or that their family will reject them if they suddenly become wealthy? What if they believe that they are bad with money and won't be able to hang onto it and that their situation will actually get worse if they become prosperous?

An even more poignant question that lurks in the subconscious stems from the fact that many base their very identities on their problems. They're so deeply ingrained that it's hard for these people to imagine themselves living a different way. If a person with money problems suddenly has money, then who will he or she *be?*

This prospect creates a potential identity crisis that many fear facing, and so they continually sabotage their own efforts to acquire wealth so as to hang on to their sense of self. This is the Ego at work. The Ego hates change, and has a very powerful influence over your actions because most of the time you don't even realize it's at work. You simply feel fear, and choose not to step through it. The Ego is satisfied, but your life stays the same . . . and thus your soul still feels the yearning to become something more.

Because we all have varied backgrounds, we have different types and levels of resistance. I've used money as an example here, but for some people resistance lies in limiting beliefs about relationships. Still others have resistance around their health. It all depends on what we witnessed around us as we were growing up.

It's also important to understand that as soon as our belief systems begin to form, our vibrational frequency is affected, and thus we begin to attract more evidence that our belief system is true. If our beliefs serve us and promote creative self-expression, feelings of self-worth, and abundance, then it's good that we are attracting in alignment with our beliefs! If, however, we were surrounded by feelings of lack, inhibition, or shame, then attracting more of this sets us up for a fairly unhappy and unrewarding experience of life.

I invite you now to look at your current circumstances and be brutally honest with yourself about whether or not they are an accurate reflection of your belief systems. I'm not talking about what you *want* to believe, what you think you *should* believe, or even what you *say* you believe. I'm talking about what you truly believe at your core.

It's entirely possible that you're not even connected with your core belief system and are therefore convinced that what you say you believe are actually your beliefs. If your reality is not in alignment with those beliefs, then I assure you that there is resistance running on some level that needs to be addressed if your situation is ever going to change.

As I've established earlier in this chapter, resistance is simply a reality in our culture. We are bombarded with negative message and "reminders" of our alleged limitations as humans. We are constantly being told what is and is not possible by people who either believe in those limitations for themselves or have reason to shape our thinking about ourselves so that they can maintain some level of control over us. This control can be governmental, societal, religious, parental, or take any number of other forms.

What you need to know is that any perception of limitation is an illusion, no matter how real it seems or how deeply you believe it. We live in a Universe of infinite possibility, and as a part of that Universe, we have direct access to an enormous amount of power to create change in our lives. We were born with this ability. It is a gift from the creative intelligence that put this Universe into motion.

It's time we learned how to shed these ideas of limitation that have been forced upon us for countless generations so that we can open the energetic channels to receive anything and everything we can imagine.

It all starts with getting crystal clear on what you truly want in your life, which isn't always as easy as one might think. Sometimes we're very clear on what our passions are, and what we want our lives to look like. Sometimes we *think* we know what we want, but we're actually chasing the dreams that someone else implanted in us based on what *they* thought we should want. We can be completely disconnected for a wide variety of reasons, some of which we'll be exploring later in this book. More importantly, in the sections that follow, we'll be sharing ways to reestablish that connection!

Chapter 2

WHAT IS YOUR VISION?

Hold Your Vision

You probably have heard the phrase "hold your vision" before, but I want to present what is possibly a different way to look at it.

The word "hold" can be interpreted a couple of different ways.

One way may cause the idea of "holding your vision" to seem like more work—an effort. Like if you don't "hold on to it," it could slip away.

You hear "hold on for dear life" . . . "hold on or you'll fall" . . . "what's the holdup?"

None of these phrases have very pleasant emotional associations, and I think that all too often the idea of "holding your vision" becomes an act of will-power rather than inspiration.

I invite you to look at other connotations of the word "hold."

Hold hands.

Hold me.

Hold a puppy or a baby.

What if you held you vision like you held a baby? With love, awe, and an immense sense of caretaking? What if holding your vision simply meant nurturing it with love and other positive feelings?

Your vision is your very life.
Your vision determines your path.

Adore your vision, and hold it dear—but not for dear life. Don't hold your vision because you believe that it can be taken away if you don't. Instead hold your vision because doing so puts you in a space of love, passion, and inspiration . . . inspiration that calls you into action along your chosen path.

The purpose of this section is to create a crystal-clear vision of what you truly want to attract into your life, making sure that this vision is based on your true sense of purpose and passion. It is much easier to stay the course when you are 100 percent certain *why* you actually have a particular goal.

I want to first review and expand upon some of the principles from chapter 1 that are going to be important to remember as you move forward.

The Law of Attraction isn't a tool. It's not a personal development technique.

The Law of Attraction is a principle of physics that explains how Energy works—more specifically, how Energy "attracts" and "repels."

We are a Universe composed of Energy. That means Everything is Energy. You, me, the dog, and the dog's thoughts. All Energy.

It is a complete illusion that we are separate from one another, as we are all connected through Energy.

This "cluster" of Energy that we call our "selves" (our body, our spirit, etc.) is configured in such a way that we interpret Energy through this gift we have of our senses. We can hear, taste, see, feel, and smell Energy in the various forms that it takes through our perception of reality.

We are able to manipulate this Energy in such a way that we occur as separate entities that are interacting with a physical Universe. In truth, this is just an interpretation of electrical signals—Energy. We truly do create our reality every moment through how we interpret Energy.

What we're only just now learning is how much control we have over how we interact with Energy.

Imagine that everything in your world is really just a hologram—a projection of light that represents the "real thing" and manifests in a very photorealistic way.

In a way, our "reality" is just like that. Everything that we perceive as physical is really just Energy—space, in essence. But our senses interpret that Energy to be something "out there"—a couch, a Chihuahua, an ukulele, or whatever.

I reiterate all of this in hopes that you can get a sense of our true Energetic nature. Because when you understand fully that you and everything are Energy, you can begin to appreciate the vast intelligence behind the fact that we even exist—let alone the full implications of our existence—and what we may be capable of.

But even though I believe we're just scratching the surface of human potential, we do have immediate access to some pretty extraordinary gifts already, many of which we rarely use, but that are capable of creating our lives like writing a script for a movie.

We've been gifted with the ability to create things that aren't yet a part of our experience through our *imagination.* We have *desires* and *dreams.*

Why do you suppose we have those? They exist for us to experience them!

An amazing intelligence created the human being with our entire range of emotions—and some of those emotions clearly feel better than others. We are naturally guided to thoughts that will make us feel better, and when each of us follows these thoughts, we begin tap into our sense of passion and purpose.

We are designed to follow our passions.

Every response in our bodies tells us that living inside a feeling of passion is *good*. And yet we are often taught to fight against that natural tendency early in life. We are *taught* what is good and bad, possible and impossible, right and wrong. If our passions don't fall in line with those things, we are often sidetracked from our passions at a very early age and we begin creating paths for ourselves with no significant intention or direction.

Remember that the Law of Attraction is *always* responding to our emotions and delivering things that are in vibrational resonance with where we are energetically.

When you have a thought and an emotional response, your body responds energetically as well as chemically. While the chemicals your body creates may cause you to feel sad in a certain situation, your overall vibration changes to one of sadness as well, and you are more in resonance with things that are sad than with things that are happy.

So until something happens to change your vibration when you've gotten into upset, it's going to be harder to attract things that are positive and helpful.

Just being aware that your thoughts are this powerful can change your life dramatically. If you become aware that negative thoughts are only going to resonate with negative situations, and that the more you dwell in a negative space, the more negative things you're going to attract, then you can make the *choice* to feel something else.

Granted, changing gears from a very negative space to a very positive space is not always easy and can feel unnatural if you try to force it by deciding to just "be happy." However, there are numerous ways to shift emotionally without it feeling forced or fake.

First, you can engage in an activity that will naturally change your state of being. This can be anything—taking a walk, playing a musical instrument, petting a dog. Engaging in virtually any kind of creative activity can create a positive effect on your vibration.

You can also change your state dramatically by moving powerfully into action on your dreams, and by learning how to release the feelings associated with that negative space, along with years of limiting beliefs. Later we'll learn specific techniques to do just that.

The beauty of being a human knowledgable about the Law of Attraction is that we get to fully *be* the creative beings we were meant to be. When we understand how the Law of Attraction works and how our deepest thoughts and feelings can cause it to behave, we can actually bring forth into physical reality things that were nothing more than seeds planted in our imaginations.

Many people spend a lot of time trying to get the Law of Attraction to "work" in their lives, and with mixed results.

Most of the time it is because they don't have an understanding of how powerfully resistance is playing a role. Resistance has a significant effect on what we are able to attract when we are intentionally utilizing the Law of Attraction. If we have Energy within us that is running powerfully at a subconscious level, it will affect our ability to get into resonance with what we truly do want, because the various energies just don't mesh. Resistance quite literally acts like an energetic force field against what you want.

In a future chapter, you will learn about tools to help you eliminate that energetic resistance so that you can begin eliminating energetic blocks to the life you desire.

Interestingly, when you are fully living a life of passion and purpose, the Law of Attraction works the way you want it to without effort or any conscious consideration that it's even part of the equation. I added "the way you want it to" because obviously the Law of Attraction is at work *all* the time, but if we've got resistance in certain areas, it can show up in ways we don't enjoy.

Living in a state of passion automatically puts you into vibrational resonance with exactly what you want . . . and you don't even have to *think* about the Law of Attraction if you don't want to. This is why you'll see many people who live amazing lives who have no knowledge at all about the Law of Attraction. They simply spend most of their time in a vibrational state that naturally attracts the good stuff. But when you get stuck, understanding the Law of Attraction and how resistance is at work can help you get back in motion instead of giving up on your dream.

Chapter 3

WE TRULY GET TO CHOOSE

The path that you follow in life is ultimately an energetic creation that you bring into being through moving into vibrational resonance with it, either consciously or unconsciously.

Ideally, of course, you'd like to do this consciously. You'd like to actually shape your destiny so that your life is in alignment with those things about which you are passionate. Notice that I said "things." I stress that word because this is not about struggling to determine your "one true passion or purpose." Your life will be filled with many of both.

I believe that years of people's lives are lost to this act of "seeking their purpose," as if they have only one chance to get it right, and if they don't do what they were divinely meant to do (some *one* thing), that they will have gotten it wrong . . . whatever they believe to be "it."

If that were true, I believe we would have been designed a lot differently than we are, both intellectually and creatively. If we were truly only here to do one thing, my belief is that it would not only be clear, it would be instinctive—that there would never be any confusion or suffering over it. We'd simply be doing it, like bees pollinate flowers. Bees pollinate because that's what they do. They don't ponder their destiny, they just *be* it.

But as humans, we get to choose, and a lot of us have a hard time with that!

The only reason we have doubt about our passion or purpose is that we feel like we should clearly be able to identify it as such.

Why should this matter?

Why can't we do something just because we enjoy it? Does it have to qualify as our "purpose" for us to commit significant time and Energy to it, or for us to assign it any real value?

The bottom line is this: whatever your vision—whatever your dream—it's going to come easier when you're truly enjoying what you're doing. Everything will seem more fun. Action will produce more profound results. You'll be surrounded by people who support you. You will begin to experience the wonder of life more than ever before.

What we want to accomplish right now is creating a starting point. We want to create a vision that inspires you into some kind of action.

You're going to create a vision that inspires you to realize your own personal greatness, while at the same time, transforming you into a powerful source of value in the world. And in return, the Universe will bring you all you need to perpetuate that experience.

Do you already have a clear vision of what you want your life to be? Great! But even so, I want you to approach this just like those who may not be so clear on what they want their lives to look like. Why? Because we want to be absolutely sure that this vision you have is truly *yours*.

I can't tell you how many times I've worked with people who are having difficulty attracting what they want, only to eventually find out that what they thought they wanted did not actually originate within themselves.

Perhaps they were "taught" early in life that they wanted to be a doctor . . . or a housewife . . . or whatever! Without really checking in with their own sense of passion, they started down a path of education and life experience that was all about creating a life as someone who wasn't even truly who they were.

This happens to a tremendous amount of people, and results in the eventuality of waking up one day feeling somewhat lost and disconnected from any sense of joy of just being who you are. Ideally, we should be celebrating who we are each and every moment . . . but we rarely do that. In too many cases, we instead remind ourselves of who we are *not*, and what we've done wrong.

But this is all the result of societal conditioning. The whole idea that we're "not good enough" was created by others who wanted people in their sphere of influence to "know their place." For an entity to stay in power, there must be some perception that this power actually exists, and that some people have it and some people don't. There are always people with reason to teach people a limited nature, rather than an unlimited one. This results in the "I can't" mentality many of us are dealing with today.

Regardless of what we're learning about the infinite nature of the Universe and the miracle that is every aspect of life, we still insist on focusing on our limitations instead of embracing the magic that it is to be human.

Here's the truth:
We absolutely get to choose our path.

It might not always be easy, particularly at first. We are talking about an approach to life that is vastly different than most of us were taught to pursue. It's an approach that says "you can do anything when it is really your desire to do so."

Creating your path can be very challenging. You're forced to think bigger than you've thought before, more consistently than you have before.

When you start to create this path, the limiting beliefs and negative thoughts will come screaming at you if your vision is not in alignment with those beliefs. Rather than try to fight those feelings, you'll instead want to recognize them for what they are: simply a learned response to a thought. The more you try to fight these feelings, the more powerful they become.

When you begin to hear the voices say "you can't do that" or "how will you do that" or "it's too big," take a moment to detach from the emotion that is triggered by those words and contemplate where they may have originated.

Did a parent or teacher or some other authority figure tell you that you "couldn't?" You believed them, of course, because why wouldn't you? But think about this: How can anyone who isn't you know what *you* are capable of? No one knows you 100 percent. We have a hard time knowing *ourselves* 100 percent, so from what position of authority can another person truly accurately assess what we can and cannot do now or in the future?

The obvious answer is that there is no such position of authority, and yet we buy into other people's beliefs about ourselves so easily that it's frightening. We adopt those beliefs as our own, and they run so deeply that they don't even appear as "beliefs" as much as just *how things really are.*

When your lifetime of beliefs have resulted in a life that seems uninspiring and with limited potential, or even a life that seems to have a lot of potential, but you just haven't been able to budge from where you are, it can be hard to hear from someone like me that you can "create anything." You simply have no evidence to support such a statement.

The truth is, however, that your belief system hasn't allowed such evidence to become a part of your experience.

You can change that. But this is a dramatic change, and to complete such a transformation, you have to have tremendously powerful incentive. That's what this vision you are going to create needs to be.

A couple of thoughts before you get started:

1. Don't ever judge or assess your vision/ dream against anyone else's. Life is not a contest to see who has the biggest, boldest, or most honorable aspirations. You are here to live *your* life. What do you want that to be?
2. Your vision need only inspire *you*. No one else around you needs to "agree" with you before you proceed. The people who will support you will appear as you walk this path you are creating.

What it Means to BE: Your Vision Fulfilled

Early in this book, I mentioned that when I started down my career path I stepped powerfully into *being* how I wanted to live in the world, rather than being someone who was *aspiring* to "someday" attain the life I wanted.

It's critical that you understand the distinction between the two. Actually being someone you want to be has an entirely different Energy than hoping/ trying/wishing to be that someone.

The Law of Attraction dictates that you are attracting those things with which you're in vibrational resonance. So as long as who you are being is someone who "hopes to be" or "will one day" be whatever it is you're imagining, that is precisely the reality with which you will be in resonance!

Most people start with "aspiring," then after enough time has passed, or after they have done enough "work," they allow themselves to step more powerfully into actual *being,* and what they attract changes. Others never make that shift. They stay locked into the vibration of "one day this will happen if I work hard enough, or if I'm good enough."

This is why I believe we have so many musicians, artist, actors, and even entrepreneurs who never quite reach the level of success they say they want. They simply aren't *being* that they are already successful. Instead they are being held back by a deeper belief that artists should suffer for their craft or that it takes years of paying dues or a lucky break to really make it.

The sooner you can move from *"trying to be"* to actually *"being,"* the sooner you will see your desire fulfilled. It is only when you become the person you want to eventually be that you can be in resonance with what it will take to bring that into the experience of your current reality.

I remember playing with this a lot when I first started working with these principles.

Although I tell this story in my book *Wealth Beyond Reason*, it bears repeating here. I was standing in my kitchen thinking about what I would feel like if I were truly a millionaire and money was no longer an issue for me. I remember shifting from the "wouldn't it be great" feeling to the "I have it now" feeling, and it was so incredibly empowering. I was able to literally think like a person without money worries, and those thoughts created a feeling . . . one that I'd never experienced before. It felt more like "abundance" than anything I'd ever experienced.

I locked onto that feeling and made a point to try and *live* inside that feeling. As I did that, my experience of money began to change dramatically.

The only thing that will truly convince you of this is simply doing it yourself . . . and that's what walking your path is all about.

You truly have to be clear on the *feeling* that you're really going after as a result of this vision coming to fruition. It's the feeling that you maintain that is absolutely the most important; it's what is shifting you vibrationally and basically instructing that energetic magnet about what to attract.

Getting Clear On Your Passion

If you are clear on your passions, then you're just about ready to start getting intentional with creating your vision.

But what if you're *not* clear?

What if you're one of the many people I meet who feels completely disconnected from their sense of passion? What if when asked to describe your "ideal life" or "vision," you don't even know where to begin?

First, you need to know that this "disconnect" from your sense of passion is simply another form of resistance.

Many times, we stop giving attention to our passions early in life. Our traditional system of education and upbringing tends to put a child down a path on which the child has no real input.

If what you have learned about your passions are that they are "okay for a hobby but not a way to make a real living" or something similar, then it is no wonder that you have disconnected yourself from your feelings of passion. It would be too painful to live with a sense of yearning to do something you believe you cannot do, so you create the story that you "don't know what your passions are."

I'm not saying that you do this intentionally, because I don't believe you do. It's simply a kind of emotional defense mechanism. If you believe that you don't know your passions, then you don't have to take responsibility for not living them. "If only I knew my passions," you might say, "I could put this Law of Attraction stuff to work in my life and things could change." But in saying that, you affirm to yourself that you *don't* know your passions, and that story becomes more and more real to you until you truly believe that you don't have anything in your life about which you're truly passionate.

Instead of feeling bad, you have chosen to feel numb.

Clearly, there is no real power in feeling numb. You can't attract anything with numb, except more numb. There are far too many people going through life numb to their sense of passion, robbing themselves and others of the gift that they are to the world.

This idea that you don't know your passion, while it feels real right now, is an idea that you need to be willing to give up if you want to move into a fully satisfying life. We are all here to live our passions, so if you're not doing that, it's time to get started!

The following are a few things to think about to help you tap into a lost sense of passion.

What do you daydream about? When your mind wanders, there's a reason it goes where it goes. Many times our daydreams are our subconscious giving us a taste of what could be.

What would you do all day if you could do *anything* and money was not an issue for you at all? This is a very common question used to help people tap into their passions, because when you truly generate the feeling of being freed up financially, you clear the way for yourself to think about what you would *truly* like to do. But if you think about all this in terms of "will it make me money?," you are cheating yourself.

You must not judge your passions on your beliefs regarding their money-making potential. Simply living your passion fully without resistance and in a big way will take care of the money for you (provided that financial abundance is a part of your vision!).

I'll note that the answer to this question "what would you do all if you could do anything" for many people is "Nothing! I would just do nothing all day." That is a totally fair answer. I invite anyone with that response to do a lot of visualization around a day filled with doing nothing, and see how those visions naturally evolve. I submit that eventually that exercise will lead you to your passion . . .

What or who inspires you? If you can't immediately access your own sense of passion, think about what or who in the world inspires you . . . and why.

You can learn a lot about yourself by looking at how you interpret people and situations. If someone inspires you because of what they are up to in the world, could that tell you a little something about what *you* might want to be up to in the world?

If you're inspired by some kind of creative expression like art, music, film, or theater, what exactly about the experience is inspiring you? Just because you're inspired by art, for example, doesn't necessarily mean that your destiny has to be being artist.

Things that inspire us aren't always the things we're supposed to be or do. However, anything that evokes inspiration in us opens a portal to the essence of who we are.

The next time you feel inspired by anything or anyone, it may be an interesting exercise to ask yourself why you're inspired. What part of yourself is being activated in this moment? What action—however large or small—do you feel called to take?

There are entire courses available to help you discover your sense of passion, but I believe that these few questions—if honestly answered—will give you very deep insight into what you're about.

A noted expert on the subject of passion is Janet Bray Attwood, author of *The Passion Test: The Effortless Path to Discovering Your Destiny.* Janet shares her thoughts and experience with the power of passion, and provides a very simple exercise that you can do right now to help reconnect you with a sense of inspired purpose.

The One Secret to Living a Passionate Life

Contributed by Janet Bray Attwood

Ever worked in a job you just couldn't stand? That was me many years ago. My office was filled with recruiters making tens of thousands of dollars every month. Each time a placement was made for another disk drive engineer, the bell would ring. But it never rang for me. I was miserable.

One day I saw a poster for a success seminar. Something about it struck a chord.

The next day I called in sick and drove an hour and a half to the event.

Sitting up front, I listened as a beautiful, articulate woman spoke about how easy it can be to enjoy success. The speaker said you just have to find those things that light you up inside, your passions.

As I listened to this remarkable woman, I felt a growing excitement inside. This was it! This was my passion, my purpose in life—to be a speaker, like this amazing woman.

"I'll find a way to get her to hire me," I thought, "Even if I have to follow her all over the country and attend every one of her seminars."

The next day when a friend casually asked how I was doing, I answered with enthusiasm. "I've found my calling! I'm going to be a motivational speaker."

I told my friend about my plan to follow this speaker around the country until she had no choice but to hire me. The only challenge was that I was at negative in the money department. "But I know I'll manage it somehow. I just know it," I told my friend.

The next day, I was sitting with my eyes closed in meditation at the local Transcendental Meditation center when I felt small pieces of paper falling on my head. I opened my eyes to discover my friend showering me with ten hundred-dollar bills, laughing and saying "Merry Christmas, go live your dream." Was I blown away? You better believe it.

I did travel across the country and was finally hired by the woman I so admired. Today, that woman is one of my best friends, and I am living my dream of being a transformational speaker and leader.

But it's been a winding road, and along the way I've learned there is one key secret to living a happy, fulfilling, rewarding life:

"Whenever you are faced with a choice,
a decision or an opportunity,
choose in favor of your passions."

There are two parts to this. First, you have to know what you are passionate about—what it is that matters most to you in your life. That's why my business partner, Chris Attwood, and I wrote *The Passion Test: The Effortless Path to Discovering Your Destiny.* The Passion Test is a simple, yet powerful way to clarify your top passions in life. Whenever I look back to that time when my friend showered me with hundred-dollar bills, I am reminded that it's not the "how" that matters most, it's the "what." As we say in *The Passion Test:*

"When you are clear, what you want will show up in your life, and only to the extent you are clear."

When you are clear about the "what" that you choose to create in your life, then you will discover the "how," often when you are least expecting it, as I did when my friend showered me with money.

The second part of living a passionate life is to choose in favor of your passions, those things that matter most to you in your life. When you do this consistently with every significant decision you make, you will be guaranteed a passionate life.

Stewart Emery, Mark Thompson, and Jerry Porras wrote a fabulous book called *Success Built to Last: Creating a Life That Matters.* They interviewed over 300 people who have enjoyed enduring success for more than twenty years. People like former Presidents Jimmy Carter and Bill Clinton, Senator John McCain, Michael Dell, Bill Gates, Lance Armstrong, Maya Angelou and many others.

All of these very successful people had one important characteristic in common: when faced with a major decision in life, they always made their choice based on what held deep meaning for them. This is what we mean by choosing in favor of your passions. Following your passions is the key to enduring success.

Contrast that with the current state of affairs in the United States. In 2005, Harris Interactive released a study that found only 20 percent of working Americans are passionate about what they do. That means 80 percent of the population is living under the illusion that following their passions is a luxury.

In a flat world, being passionate about what you do has become a necessity for survival. Today, Jill Smith in Miami is no longer competing for her job with just the people in her local area. She is competing with people all over the world.

As Larry Bossidy, former CEO of Honeywell and Allied Signal, and author of *Execution: The Discipline of Getting Things Done,* has said: "It's a competitive imperative. Only by loving what you do will you actually do more and do it better than the person sitting next to you [or on the other side of the world]. If you don't, well then, we'll find someone who does."

The good news is that when you discover what you love and commit yourself to aligning your life with that thing, magic begins to happen. Things you thought were impossible become possible. Doors open for you.

Sometimes, when you listen to all the advice that's available about what is necessary to create a happy, fulfilling, successful life, it can be a bit overwhelming. When you boil it down, if you are able to do nothing else, clarify your passions and then choose in favor of them, and you will discover your life unfolding in exciting, new, unexpected ways.

But what if you're not clear on your passions? What if your circumstances have created a mindset within you that seems to suggest that there is no hope?

Here's an exercise that I recommend to people who I work with that is simple but tremendously powerful. It will give you the ability to shift your entire perception away from what you don't like about your current circumstances, and instead put your emotional Energy into something that can provide inspiration.

Ask yourself this simple question: What do I never want to happen in my life again?

Write down all that you can think of in response to that question. Get it all out and on paper.

Then simply write down the opposite of each item—something that you'd absolutely love to happen!

So simple, right? But try it!

For example, when I spoke to the homeless, I asked the question, "What do you never want to happen again?" and one person responded (as I'm sure many were thinking), "I never want to live on the streets again."

I then asked them to state what the opposite of that would be. "To live in a beautiful home." The shift was powerful and palpable.

Try this exercise if you feel disconnected from your sense of passion. You'll be amazed at the wave of inspiration you will create. You'll find yourself with a new sense of direction that you can immediately act upon!

I can't guarantee that you will have hundred-dollar bills showered on your head, but I can guarantee that your life will be more rewarding than you ever imagined.

Chapter 4

RELEASE TECHNIQUES

Lowering the Energetic Force Field

Before you even start becoming intentional about shifting your vibration towards alignment with your dream life, you need to be prepared to deal with the resistance that will likely show up.

The failure to have the tools to do so is what accounts for virtually all perceived failure of Law of Attraction techniques or programs. While many teachers talk of the importance of "letting go of attachment" or simply "allowing" the Universe to deliver, for the most part they do not provide specific instructions on how to do this, and any instructions that are given were vague at best.

Recently, incredible breakthroughs in understanding the human Energy system have brought forth extremely powerful tools to deal directly with resistance. Because resistance is simply Energy that is vibrating at a frequency not in resonance with what we want, we will have to actually change the vibration of that Energy. That is what release techniques facilitate.

The release techniques described here are extremely simple to use, and can be used in the moment that you are aware of the resistance. You'll know you're experiencing resistance because it is virtually always associated with a negative thought or feeling. If you have any thought that deflates your enthusiasm for your vision, then you are dealing with resistance. That moment is the best time to utilize these techniques.

I want to underline that by saying that release techniques are most effective when you use them throughout the day in the moment of any upset. They are generally not nearly as powerful when used "after the fact." The key to most release techniques is being tuned in to the emotion you want to release. Working on these emotions later in the day is generally not nearly as effective as addressing them in the moment.

Your goal should be to get to a point where you can release resistance spontaneously in any given moment. That ability will come with practice. The more you experience the feeling of releasing resistance, the easier it will be to do it spontaneously. Like our intuition and our ability to manifest our experience of reality, releasing negative Energy is something that we can naturally do, but were never taught how. Like anything else you learn, the more you do it, the better you'll become.

Imagine being able to let go of anger in an instant. What would life be like if feelings like jealousy, hatred, self-doubt, irrational fear, and worry could become only fleeting moments in your day rather than heavy emotional weights affecting your ability to live a life that you enjoy?

By definition, resistance is the only thing that is keeping you from experiencing your desire right now. Learning effective release techniques is one of the most powerful abilities you can cultivate.

Emotional Freedom Techniques

Among the most effective techniques I use and recommend are the Emotional Freedom Techniques created by Gary Craig.

Although there are many forms of this technique that can be classified as *meridian tapping*, EFT was one of the first I actually used on myself with great success.

As you learn about the technique, you may find yourself feeling a little more than skeptical, as I did. After all, in essence the process involves tapping various parts of the body while talking to yourself. I didn't even try it on myself for almost a year after learning about it, because I just couldn't grasp intellectually how it would work.

Thankfully, a colleague eventually talked me into just giving it a try the next time I found myself in a state of upset. Once I actually did the process, I immediately understood how integrating EFT into my teaching of the Law of Attraction could dramatically impact the results our students achieved.

Since that time, I have come into contact with many excellent EFT practitioners, all with unique styles, and all of them effective.

Because I consider myself an EFT enthusiast more than a practitioner, I thought it best to leave the full explanation of the process and its implementation to a true Master of the practice. I have chosen my good friend Carol Look to walk you through the history and application of this incredibly powerful process, which I consider my "go-to" release technique in just about every situation.

Emotional Freedom Techniques Contributed by Carol Look, LCSW, DCH, EFT Master

EFT is a form of psychological acupressure treatment that uses a gentle tapping technique instead of needles to stimulate traditional Chinese acupuncture points on the Energy meridians we have in our bodies. This self-help technique "borrows" the acupuncture theory that Energy gets blocked in these circuits of electricity, resulting in emotional and physical symptoms. The tapping

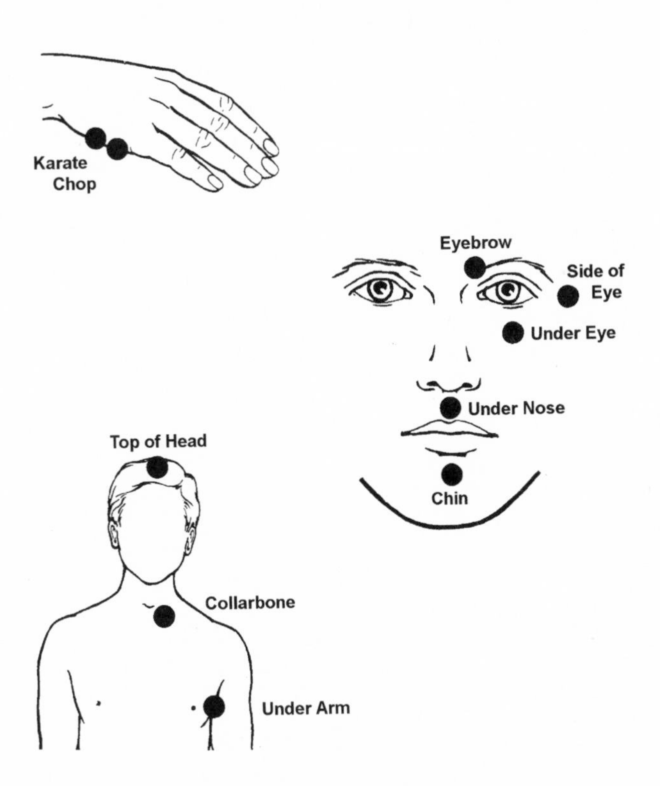

can eliminate these Energy blockages much like inserting acupuncture needles clears imbalances in the body.

Created by former engineer and personal performance coach, Gary Craig, EFT is considered one of the simpler and most effective forms of Energy Therapy. It has most of the same ingredients of its predecessor TFT, the original "tapping therapy" created by Dr. Roger Callahan in the 1980s, but it is easier to apply to oneself and others.

The Treatment: The treatment includes focus, verbalizations, and tapping on the meridian points. While a person is tuned in to an emotional problem, challenge, or ailment, he or she starts *tapping on the designated acupuncture points* on the face and body while *repeating a phrase that represents the identified problem.*

Combining these ingredients of the EFT technique—focus, verbalizations, and tapping—seems to *balance the Energy system* and relieve emotional distress and physical pain. Restoring the balance of the Energy system allows the body and mind to resume their natural healing abilities. EFT is safe, easy to apply, and is noninvasive. EFT has been used successfully for the following problems:

- Severe stress reactions
- Insomnia
- Performance anxiety
- Allergies
- Limiting beliefs/ Blocks to success and abundance
- PTSD (post-traumatic stress disorder)
- Childhood trauma
- Pain relief
- Mild to severe anxiety (including phobias)
- Food, sugar. cigarette, and chemical cravings
- And many more . . .

I have been trained in several of the "tapping modalities" since 1997, and continue to be astounded by the ongoing successes that I, my clients, and workshop participants enjoy when using EFT.

EFT can be viewed as a kind of "recipe" with several key ingredients. Although the basic ingredients are simple and have not been modified for nearly two decades, practitioners who have training in other modalities naturally improvise and combine EFT with other tools. Below is my slight modification of the original treatment protocol.

For EFT to be effective, you need to:

1. Choose a clear target.
2. Aim the EFT tapping treatment at the target.
3. Follow up with tapping on additional aspects of the problem.

Your "target" is the problem you have chosen to work on with the tapping of EFT. Your target may be a belief, an emotion, an event, a craving, or a pain in your body. Below are examples of typical targets for EFT treatment.

1. Belief: *"I don't have what it takes to be successful."*
2. Emotion: *"I feel so anxious about Monday's meeting."*
3. Event: *"The time my father humiliated me in public."*
4. Craving: *"I always crave sugar late in the afternoon."*
5. Pain: *"I have this sharp pain in my lower back."*

The basic ingredients of the EFT recipe are:

The Setup Statement: After choosing the target to work on, we begin with the Setup Statement, (naming the problem combined with a general affirmation phrase). A Setup Statement sounds like this:

"Even though I have this anxiety about the meeting with my boss, I deeply and completely love and accept myself."

The Setup Statement is repeated out loud three times while you tap the karate chop point (KC) (see diagram of points on page 61). There are dozens of variations on this original Setup Statement. The point is that the statement directs our focus to the target, while inspiring us to accept ourselves at the same time.

The Reminder Phrase: (the words you repeat out loud when you are tapping on the sequence of points) sounds like this:

"This anxiety about the meeting with my boss."

The Reminder Phrase is repeated when you tap the sequence of tapping points. It helps you tune in and stay focused on the issue you have chosen for treatment.

Negative Tapping Round: (Round #1): This consists of tapping the sequence of eight EFT "power points" while you *focus on the problem* and say the *Reminder Phrase* out loud. (This helps you *tune in* to the problem.)

Starting at the eyebrow point, begin tapping each point in the sequence of points (see page 66) approximately seven to ten times while repeating the *negative Reminder Phrase.*

Sequence of EFT Tapping Points:

- Eyebrow (EB)
- Side of Eye (SE)
- Under Eye (UE)
- Under Nose (UN)
- Chin (CH)
- Collarbone (CB)
- Under Arm (UA)
- Top of Head (H)

This directs your mind to focus on the negative thought patterns that block your ability to reach your goals (feel calm, attract abundance, or release food cravings) and *allows EFT to neutralize them*.

Positive Tapping Sequence: (Round #2): Tap on the sequence of the eight EFT power points again, and *focus on a solution* by verbalizing preferences, choices, and possible alternative outcomes. Starting at the eyebrow point again, tap each of the eight points approximately seven to ten times while *repeating any sequence of positive phrases* you choose.

This allows you to install what you would *prefer* to experience emotionally in your thought patterns and in your life.

Deep Breath: Complete each exercise with a slow deep breath to help move the released Energy through your body.

In summary:

Simple EFT Directions

- Choose a feeling, belief, or pain to target with EFT.
- Rate the intensity "charge" on the zero to tenzero to ten point scale.
- Devise the Setup Statement.
- Form your Reminder Phrase.
- Tap on the sequence of eight points, *focusing on the problem.*
- Tap on the sequence of eight points, *focusing on a solution.*
- Take a deep breath.
- Measure the intensity "charge" on the zero to ten point scale again.
- Tap again if necessary to continue reducing the "charge."

The Zero-to-Ten-Point Intensity Scale: The Intensity Scale is a scale of measurement from zero to ten, where zero equals no discomfort at all, and ten equals an incredibly high rating of emotional discomfort or "charge" you feel about the issue you have identified (targeted) to work on with EFT.

EFT practitioners take the measurement before and after completing one or more rounds of EFT. You could also call the scale of measurement the "Upset Chart" or the "Truth Meter." It doesn't matter what you call it, the point is that using the Intensity Scale helps you track your progress when doing EFT so you are able to measure the "before and after" results.

The Intensity Scale can be used to measure a variety of responses:

- *How true* does the belief feel on the zero to ten point scale?
- *How intense* is your discomfort from zero to ten?
- *How true* does this *statement* feel to you on the zero to ten point scale?
- *How upset* do you feel about this event?
- *How anxious* are you about this issue?

I always ask my clients to measure their number on the scale from their gut feeling, not from an intellectual perspective. I want to hear how high or low the actual *feeling* and *rating* is on the scale, not what they think it "should" or "shouldn't" feel like.

EFT Tapping Points
Sample EFT Exercise

Measure the "charge" of this fear on the zero to ten point scale. While tapping on your Karate Chop Point (KC) on either hand, repeat the following Setup Statement three times:

Even though I'm afraid to be successful,
I deeply and completely love and accept myself.

Tap the sequence of eight points while repeating the Negative Reminder Phrase, "I'm afraid to be successful" (or alternate the wording as in the below example. Either way is acceptable and effective).

Round #1: Negative Tapping Sequence

(eyebrow)	This deep fear of being successful . . .
(side of eye)	I'm afraid to be successful . . .
(under eye)	I'm afraid they'll hurt me if I'm successful . . .
(under nose)	I'm afraid to be successful . . .
(chin)	I have this deep fear of being successful . . .
(collarbone)	I'm afraid to be successful . . .
(under arm)	I've had this fear for a long time . . .
(head)	I'm afraid to be successful.

Then perform The Positive Tapping Sequence (Round #2) with positive words reflecting your desired outcome. Repeat one phrase for each of the eight tapping points from the Eyebrow (EB) to the Top of the Head (H). You may repeat the same phrase over and over again, or vary the phrases as you wish.

Round #2: Positive Tapping Sequence

(eyebrow)	I love knowing I can let go of this fear . . .
(side of eye)	I choose to release this conflict about success . . .
(under eye)	It feels so right to feel good about success . . .
(under nose)	I appreciate that success is good for us all . . .
(chin)	I love knowing I can be safe and successful . . .
(collarbone)	I choose to release this conflict about success . . .
(under arm)	It feels so right to be free of this conflict . . .
(head)	I love attracting abundance and being successful.

Measure the "charge" on the zero to ten point scale again.

Repeat as necessary.

Carol Look is a success and abundance coach in the Energy psychology field. Her specialty is inspiring clients to attract abundance into their lives by using EFT/Meridian Tapping and the Law of Attraction to clear limiting beliefs, release resistance, and build "prosperity consciousness." Before becoming an EFT Master, Carol was trained as a Clinical Social Worker and earned her Doctoral Degree in Clinical Hypnotherapy.

A pioneer and leading voice in the EFT community, Carol is well known for her four seasons as an Internet radio show host and as the author of the popular books, *Attracting Abundance with EFT* and *Improve Your Eyesight with EFT.* She has also produced several audio CD sets and downloadable programs on attracting abundance, weight loss, clearing clutter, and fear of public speaking, as well as DVDs on the topics of attracting abundance and healing pain and illness. Carol appears as a practitioner and Energy therapy expert in the DVD documentary *The Tapping Solution* as well as in the documentary focusing on helping veterans suffering from PTSD, *Operation: Emotional Freedom.*

Carol has closed her private practice in order to focus on writing and recording new training products and teaching live EFT/Meridian Tapping workshops to practitioners and laypeople around the world.

Disclaimer

EFT is an experimental therapy, and is not meant to replace standard medical and/or mental health counseling. While there have been no documented negative side effects from using EFT when the proper treatment protocols have been followed, this does *not* mean that you will not experience side effects. By using these techniques on yourself or others, you must agree to take full responsibility for your own well-being and you must advise your clients to do the same. Please consult your health care practitioner before beginning any new program.

The Sedona Method

Almost from the time I started studying personal development, I heard a lot about the Sedona Method. This was many years before I knew anything of the Law of Attraction, and thus the idea of "releasing negative emotions" didn't hold my interest. After all, I didn't see how simply feeling better emotionally was going to have any impact on my quest for abundance!

Once I learned how the Law of Attraction really worked, that all changed. When I began to understand the impact that negative thoughts and beliefs were having on my ability to attract what I wanted into my life, I began looking for processes to deal with those emotions, and it wasn't long before The Sedona Method showed up on my radar once again.

This time, however, I pursued a full understanding of the process by going straight to its creator, Hale Dwoskin. Hale was also featured in *The Secret* and I had the absolutely pleasure of meeting him personally a couple of years after the film was released. Hale is an extraordinary human being in nearly every sense of the word, and a true testament to the power of The Sedona Method. When you're in his presence your Energy changes in a significant way, as he simply exudes peace in a way that you don't experience with most people.

I asked Hale to share The Sedona Method with you in this book so that you can experience its transformative effects for yourself. Don't be fooled by its simplicity like many are when they initially learn how the process works. Instead, just try it for yourself and see why it is among my most highly recommended release techniques.

Introduction to the Sedona Method Contributed by Hale Dwoskin

One of the main ways that we create disappointments, unhappiness, and misjudgments is by holding on to limiting thoughts and feelings. It is not that "holding on" in and of itself is inappropriate. Holding on is perfectly appropriate in many situations. I wouldn't suggest, for instance, that you not hold on to the steering wheel of a car that you were driving, or not hold on to a ladder that you were climbing. Obviously, the results of such choices could be unfortunate. But have you ever held on to a point of view even when it didn't serve you? Have you ever held on to an emotion, even though there was nothing you could do to satisfy it, make it right, or change the situation that appeared to cause it? Have you ever held on to tension or anxiety even after the initial event that triggered it was long over?

The momentum of your habitual ways of thinking, feeling, and behaving may often have you feeling like you are trying to move forward with a rubber band around your waist. Even when you're very close to attracting what you want into your life, the pull of your old reactions is so strong that you seem to snap back into your old patterns.

These patterns are stealing your Energy. Every negative pattern you are holding onto from the past is robbing you of the Energy that you could be using to create all that you choose.

Now here's a thought about thinking to ponder: If you truly have over 50,000 thoughts a day, that's a lot of thoughts to try to control and make positive. Yet if you "wake up on the wrong side of the bed," you can have the same *feeling* the whole day coloring every thought. So it is much more effective to *master your emotions* than simply trying to *control your thoughts*.

So, how do you use the Law of Attraction in your life to produce the results you want?

Well, what is the opposite of holding on? "Letting go," of course. Both letting go and holding on are part of the natural process of life. This fundamental understanding is the basis of The Sedona Method. No matter who you are, if you're reading these words, I can guarantee that you've already frequently experienced letting go, often without being aware that it was happening—and even without being taught the Method.

Have you ever watched a very young child fall down and then look around to see if there is any reason to be upset? When children think no one is watching them, in an instant they just let go, brush themselves off, and act like nothing has happened.

The same child in a similar situation, on seeing the opportunity to get attention, may burst into tears and run to the arms of a parent. This natural ability to release our emotions was lost to most of us because, even though we did it automatically as young children, without conscious control, our parents, teachers, friends, and society as a whole trained us out of it as we got older.

Letting go is a natural ability that we're all born with, but which we get conditioned against using as we mature into adulthood. Where so many of us frequently get stuck is that we don't know when it is appropriate to let go and when it is appropriate to hold on. And most of us err on the side of holding on—often to our detriment.

When you let go of your negative patterns, you can then channel this Energy into your worthy goals and intentions.

Remember, to create what you want, it is important to *feel* that you already have what you want and not just think it. There is no more effective way to let go of your negative emotions and feel the positive outcome of your goals than with The Sedona Method.

But what about subconscious thoughts and feelings?

Well, you are creating the sum total of your thinking and feeling about any particular topic all the time, but most of thinking and feeling is below your conscious awareness in your subconscious. In fact, 94–96 percent of your actions are motivated by the thoughts and feelings that are outside of your conscious awareness and control. The good news is that when you let go of your *conscious* feelings using The Sedona Method, you also empty your *subconscious* and you take back your control.

Letting go of your thoughts and feelings actually dissolves the negative emotional charge and allows you to easily feel the natural feelings of joy, peace, happiness, wealth, and love that are your true nature. You can let go of anything negative and uncover the positive that is natural in each and every one of us at our core. This will quickly and dramatically shift your sum total thinking and feeling about your goals and dreams and allow you to put the Law of Attraction into full effect in your life.

Here is a very simple but deceptively powerful letting go exercise you can start to experiment with in your own life:

What is your NOW feeling?
Could you welcome/allow that feeling?
Could you let it go?
Would you let it go?
When?

These are the five basic releasing questions that serve as the foundation of The Sedona Method. Here is how to apply them on your own. Experiment with asking the questions both in the first person and in the third person and find which works best for you.

Step 1: Focus on an issue that you would like to feel better about, and then allow yourself to feel whatever you are feeling in this moment.

Ask yourself: *What is my NOW feeling about this topic?*

This doesn't have to be a strong feeling. In fact, you can even check on how you feel about this exercise and what you want to get from it.

Step 2: Welcome the feeling, as well as any sensations, sounds, thoughts, and pictures that arise with the feeling, and allow whatever you are experiencing to be here as fully or as best you can.

Ask yourself: *Could I allow myself to welcome this feeling?*

This instruction may seem simplistic, but it needs to be.

Most of us live in our thoughts, pictures, and stories about the past and the future, rather than being aware of how we actually feel in the moment. The only time that we can actually do anything about the way we feel (and, for that matter, about our businesses or our lives) is *now*. You don't need to wait for a feeling to be strong or to have a label before you let it go.

In fact, if you are feeling numb, flat, blank, cut off, or empty inside, those are feelings that can be let go just as easily as more recognizable ones. Simply do the best you can.

Step 3: Ask yourself: *Could I let this feeling go?*

This question is merely asking you if it is possible to take this action. "Yes" or "no" are both acceptable answers. You will often let go even if you answer "no." As best you can, answer the question with a minimum of thought, staying away from second-guessing yourself or getting into an internal debate about the merits of that action or its consequences.

All the questions used in this process are deliberately simple. They are not important in and of themselves but are designed to point you to the experience of letting go, to the experience of stopping holding on. Go on to Step 4 no matter how you answered this question.

Step 4: No matter which question you started with, ask yourself this simple question: *Would I?* In other words: Am I willing to let go?

Again, stay away from debate as best you can. Also remember that you are always doing this process for yourself, for the purpose of gaining your own freedom and clarity. It doesn't matter whether the feeling is justified, longstanding, or right.

If the answer is "no," or if you are not sure, ask yourself:

"Would I rather have this feeling, or would I rather be free?"

Even if the answer is still "no," go on to Step 5.

Step 5: Ask yourself a simpler question: *When?*

This is an invitation to just let it go now. You may find yourself easily letting go. Remember that letting go is a decision you can make any time you choose.

Step 6: Repeat the preceding five steps as often as needed until you feel free of the particular feeling with which you started the process.

Note: If you are having a hard time deciding to let go or simply feeling a difference, then you can also give yourself permission to hold on for a moment. If you give yourself permission to do what you are already doing, you will find that it becomes much easier to make a new decision. This will usually make getting to a genuine "yes" and the corresponding letting go much easier.

You will probably find yourself letting go a little more on each step of the process. The results at first may be quite subtle. Very quickly, if you are persistent, the results will get more and more noticeable. You may find that you have layers of feelings about a particular topic. However, what you let go of is gone for good.

You can learn more about Hale Dwoskin and The Sedona Method in the Resources section on page 229.

Chapter 5

VISUALIZATION

Visualization is really the first step in the manifestation process. After all, the moment we get a notion that we want something, some kind of image or idea forms in our head. It is the symbol of what we want to attain. For that image to manifest into your reality, it must cause the energetic shift in your vibration that happens when you have an emotional response.

If you can generate the same emotions you will have when your desire is fulfilled, you align vibrationally with the reality of the fulfilled desire and thus become a magnet to it.

Please reread the last sentence. It basically means that by simply experiencing the emotion of having your desire fulfilled, you begin to draw the *reality* of those feelings to you through the Law of Attraction.

This requires some degree of visualization. That does not necessarily mean that you have to "see images" in your imagination, although that helps immensely. Through visualizing what it is like to have your desire fulfilled, your mind and body actually respond physically in an emotional way. That is, you change your vibration. You can actually feel it if you even slightly tune into it.

As you visualize, or imagine, you want to conjure up a reaction from every one of your five senses—as well as those senses, like emotion, that are less tangible.

You want to *see, hear, feel, smell, and taste* your desire being fulfilled. And the key is to *stay in that state as consistently as possible.* This is where visualization exercises come into play. This simply means that you are intentionally bringing forth mental imagery in order to shift your vibration.

As you go through the process of creating your vision, emotional responses will be evoked. That is the purpose of visualization. Not all of them will be 100 percent positive, however.

Positive or negative, an honest look at your emotional responses to a vision that is designed to evoke inspiration can tell you a lot about whether or not you're on the right track with the creation of your vision.

Sometimes in exercises like these, we will write down answers or create mental images we *think* we should have. For example, if we're imagining great financial wealth, we may write down that we feel abundant when we visualize our future—when it may be that in the present we don't feel abundant at all.

It's crucial that we be honest with ourselves about our feelings. Again, these emotions are real Energy, with true attractive power—and they don't magically go away when you ignore them or push them down. We have to actually transform those Energy patterns into something else so that they don't act as that energetic force field against the experience of life we're trying to have.

Maybe you don't really want a million dollars. In fact, you may have some very strong negative feelings about that amount of money. You might have thoughts like, "it would be too hard to get," or "too hard to keep," or even ideas like "people with that kind of money are bad or shallow."

With those types of beliefs running, it's no wonder people often sabotage themselves when it comes to money. They try to create a vision filled with abundance, but their dysfunctional energetic relationship to money has to be addressed first.

This exercise of honestly assessing your emotional responses to your vision is what is most often *not* done when people start the process of visualizing their dream life.

As a result, they start down a path that they create, but they aren't really clear about why this is their path in the first place, or they have conflicting beliefs about the appropriateness of that path.

In this case, as in all cases, the Law of Attraction works perfectly every time, bringing them situations that are in resonance with their confusion or ambiguity, and what results is the experience that this "vision" thing doesn't work at all.

If you really go through these exercises this won't be the case for you.

This process will get you crystal clear on the correct path for *you* before you take your first step. In this way, you'll know that the circumstances that occur in front of you on your journey are completely appropriate and there to guide you in the proper direction. You'll know that the "voices" you hear are intuitive nudges rather than the voices of resistance and limited thinking.

Most importantly, you'll know how to recognize a change in direction when it's appropriate.

The path you feel guided to follow is an outgrowth of universal intelligence—an intelligence far greater than I believe we as humans are currently configured to fully experience. But we do have access to that intelligence at any time!

When we create our path and set forth an energetic event through the act of visualization, the Universe will provide us with instructions for the next steps that are in alignment with where we are in that moment. But as we travel down our path, our vision is likely to grow and evolve into something even more inspiring.

When we become inspired to new levels, we shift emotionally, and thus vibrationally, and the Universe responds in kind. This can result in our path taking on a new direction. This is the perfect response.

This is where the concept of "going with the flow" will make all the difference. In this case, we're talking about the energetic flow, which will occur naturally in response to what we're vibrating (how we're feeling.) The flow comes to us just as it's supposed to. We can choose to "go with it" and take action according to the intuitive voices we hear in our head; we can choose to evaluate and assess ad nauseum what the voices really mean, whether or not they are truly intuition; or take any other number of intellectually based actions. This is second-guessing the Universe, and changes your vibration immediately in such a way that it will now be all up to you to figure out the correct action to take.

Isn't that what you've always done?

Another way we stop or slow our progress toward true fulfillment is by getting attached to our original ideas. We may start down the path very excited at how spontaneously it has appeared . . . but when we start to intellectualize what is coming our way, we often reach a point where we think, "Oh, I see where this is going . . ." and we try to let our intellect take over the process.

This causes a problem when the Universe provides us with a change in direction we weren't anticipating logically. We resist the change because we've already got this "all figured out." In those moments, we limit ourselves, often so much that we actually end up quitting.

You start down your path with one vision—and it will almost certainly evolve, perfectly and appropriately. The Universe is responding with infinite intelligence, but our intellect hasn't seen "the even bigger picture," and is still attached to our original vision.

When we don't allow ourselves to work in *concert* with the Universe, we aren't assured that our results are going to be in alignment with the spirit and Energy of our original vision. We may get what we were attached to, but we'll be left with a feeling of "is this all there is?" Or we may just not make much progress at all, because now we're changing the rules, taking over the job we previously gave to universal intelligence.

Another way we limit ourselves is in the vision itself. We simply don't think big enough.

My friend Sonia Ricotti, author of *The Law of Attraction, Plain and Simple*, likes to have people go through the exercise of creating their vision strongly in their minds and then multiplying whatever they are thinking about by ten. The power of that exercise is twofold. First, it will expand a person's financial set point if they do it consistently. I can attest to the power of looking at a million dollars as if it's not a lot of money. It was only when I began to think that way that I was able to receive money like that. When you multiply your original vision by ten, a lot of very deep and very powerful resistance will show itself quickly. And you'll be armed and ready for it as a result of reading this book.

A lot of this resistance spawns from some level of distrust in the process itself. After all, if we fully trusted this "reality creation" process, we would never have to judge anything that showed up as "bad." Instead, we'd see it as appropriate *somehow* (and we *don't have to know how*) with regard to us getting where we ultimately want to go.

When we have doubt in the process and we're triggered to feel negatively when a certain event occurs, we have the choice to continue with that negative feeling because it seems the most "natural" (but actually, it's just the most automatic), or we can choose to trust that whatever is happening is for the greater good.

Can that be nearly impossible for us sometimes? Absolutely. There are some situations that occur in which we as civilized human beings are not likely going to see the "greater good." Nonetheless, it is still a choice.

Again, there is no expectation that you will never have negative feelings. It's very likely that you will. We are meant to experience these emotions, or they wouldn't exist in us. But it's what we *do* with those negative feelings that is significant.

If we dwell in a negative feeling, then of course our energetic vibration is going to shift, and we will become more in resonance with things that match that negative feeling vibration.

You *can* choose to fully release the negative feeling, eliminating its charge completely using the release techniques discussed earlier.

All of this is to say that as you travel your path, it's likely that you are going to be presented with the option to create a new path completely, and that you should not necessarily resist that nudge.

I want to share some of the more effective visualization techniques you can use to start to shift your vibration. As you go through any and all of these, I urge you to take note of any negative feelings that surface and use the release technique of your choice in the moment it occurs. This will make the visualization process more effective and efficient.

Visualization through Writing

Although visualization is normally associated with closing your eyes and using your imagination, writing is actually highly effective in generating the images and feelings that will powerfully alter your vibration.

These short and simple writing exercises are designed to help you create your path, and while the steps are simple, each has a fairly complex impact on our vibration.

When you actually go through the process of completing these simple pages, you are changing your energetic structure in a very significant way. Your life *is* going to change—so be prepared for it.

Use these pages as a guide. This is an exercise you can do on a computer or on paper—wherever it's most convenient for you. We have reached a pivotal point in your experience with this book. I'm asking you to take action in the form of writing. If you're like a lot of people, you'll want to just "think" the responses to these exercises in your head, so before you do that please consider the following.

I have coached hundreds of people through this process. I cannot tell you how many emails or phone calls I get that go like this:

"Bob, I have read about all these techniques and things just aren't improving! It just is not working!"

When I ask if they've taken the time to detail things out on paper, the answer is almost always no.

Is it hard to take out a pencil and paper and write down a list of things you truly desire? You wouldn't think so, but it's amazing what a little resistance can make difficult. People still seem to believe that reading a book is the same thing as taking action regarding what they read.

This process is really a great deal of fun, once you actually start! It is like anything else, though. Starting seems to be the hardest part. Perhaps you want so much that the thought of writing it all down is overwhelming! So you keep it in your head, thinking that is good enough. For most of us it is *not*, for several reasons:

1. Writing transforms your desire from intangible thought into the physical in the form of words on paper (or a computer screen) that you can actually read.
2. Writing helps you gain clarity and further refine your desire into something you absolutely know you want.
3. Writing allows your desire to "stand alone" without being surrounded by the clutter that normally exists in our thoughts regarding what we want.

Until you actually write your thoughts down, you will never know how powerful this exercise is. Unfortunately, most people see this as much too easy and do not believe that something so simple can bring them what they want.

I am often asked how detailed one must get with this writing. What matters most is that the process of putting pen to paper gets you into a vibration that is in resonance with *having* those things about which you are writing. If you know anything about affirmations—positive statements that reflect changes you'd like to make in your life—you know that you always want to write these statements in the present, rather than future tense. For example, instead of:

"I want a new car."

You would write:

"I have a new car."

But to really be effective, you want to go further. You need to express *emotion* in your words, because by doing so you will invoke the desired emotion within yourself, thus shifting your vibration toward *being* that you have that car, rather than being that you *want* that car.

"I am exhilarated each time I step into my dream car."

"I love the smell of the soft, clean leather that fills my senses as I drive."

Do you see how those statements evoke much more of an emotional response than "I want a new car?" The more detailed you are in your writing, the more likely you are to get into the exact vibrational state you want in order to attract what you are writing about.

But what if every time you write a statement like that, you feel like you're lying to yourself? What if you are confronted with the "fact" that the statements you are writing are not true? You might feel a wave of very negative emotion, and that is certainly something you do not want to sustain, right?

That negative emotion is an indication of resistance; a tell-tale sign that your current belief system is not in harmony with what you are writing.

Let's begin. Use the pages that follow as a guide to create something similar in a notebook you will use for this and other writing exercises.

Describe a day in your ideal life. Include your overall emotional state, and be as descriptive as possible. Start from the time you wake up in the morning until you go to bed. Really include the details of what you're *doing*, not just vague generalizations that you can't generate pictures with.

Describe WHY the preceding is your "ideal" life. How do you express who you truly are through what you have described?

Explain why you can NOT stop until you've realized your vision. Your vision should be highly compelling, and should call to you at a deep level. Address this question as if someone had told you to stop walking this path for some reason, and you are responding here as to why that is simply not an option.

When you really focus on your vision (generating realistic pictures, sounds, smells, etc. as if it's all already come to pass), what feelings honestly come up for you? These can be negative or positive thoughts and feelings, but try to list them all in both categories.

Positive Feelings	Negative Feelings
"I feel so alive!"	"I don't deserve this . . . "

Other Visualization Techniques

The writing exercises in the last section are a form of visualization technique, and you can do them over and over to refine your vision. With time, this will be an automatic process, and you won't have to write everything down!

I acknowledge that for some, writing can feel cumbersome, and while I'm clearly a fan of utilizing writing to clarify your vision, there are numerous other ways to shift your vibration. I will share some of the more common techniques here.

The Vision Board

This is a very popular technique for clarifying what you want to be a part of your life experience. When you're done you have a visual aid that you can refer to throughout your day to generate those positive feelings of "having it now."

Although your vision board can take whatever form you'd like, the basic idea is to create some kind of visual collage that represents the things you want to fill your life. This can be pictures of actual "stuff" like cars, homes, and money. You can also use images that represent certain feelings you'd like to have, such as love, peace, and health.

The sole purpose of the vision board, and truly any visualization technique, is to generate a positive emotional state that is in alignment with what you truly want your life to become. If your vision board is not doing that, then it's impotent. Just as in the writing exercise, you want to be aware of any negative emotions that surface as you create your vision board. These would be thoughts like, "I'll never get that!" or "How could that ever happen to someone like me" or "This is silly. This will never work."

These are all thoughts indicative of resistance that needs to be addressed through release techniques.

Ideally, your vision board should be placed somewhere where you will see it frequently so that the amount of time you are vibrating in resonance with what you want is significant.

If you work at a computer for extended amounts of time, you might consider creating a digital vision board. As mentioned earlier, I did a form of this when I first started working with the Law of Attraction and had great results. Not only did I make significant changes to my bank account by using a "tweaked" image of my bank statement as my computer's background wallpaper, but I used the same process to manifest both a car and exercise equipment that I wanted!

Currently, there are several vision board software programs available on the Internet that allow the easy creation of images and even screen savers complete with sound to enhance the sensory stimulation even more. If you don't feel that you have the patience to sift through magazines and cut out images to create a traditional vision board, you might check the Recommended Resources listed at the end of this book and consider these programs as an alternative.

Meditation

Meditation, while used for many purposes across many disciplines, is an excellent way for you to accelerate the manifestation process.

Meditation allows you to quiet the mind so that it is easier for you to direct your attention as you wish, rather than being bombarded by a lot of noise and screaming from the Ego that "You can't possibly have all these things you want!"

Meditation techniques abound. You can find them everywhere. Some are as simple as merely putting your attention towards counting your breaths while seated in a comfortable position.

But for those with really noisy minds and who are in a hurry, there are alternatives.

There is a technology called "brainwave synchronization" that can be embedded in recorded audio that actually induces the meditative state in the listener with no effort on their part.

There are also hardware alternatives such as "light and sound goggles" that help to induce the meditative state.

Meditation audio CDs are available in practically any book and music store, any number of which can help guide you into a mental frame of mind suitable for powerful visualization.

Use whichever approach works best for you. While in the meditative state (depending on how deep you go), your visualization ability will greatly enhanced, and you will find that it is much easier to "be" that your desire has been fulfilled!

Because the whole goal is to move yourself into vibrational resonance with what you want to attract, we have created an exercise called "The Experiential Meditation." See the "Recommended Resources" section of the book for information on how to obtain a recorded version of this meditation produced by Boundless Living at no charge.

The Experiential Meditation

This purpose of this meditation is to put you powerfully into vibrational resonance with the vision you have created by doing the work in this book. Rather than focusing on trying to attract a specific thing such as a car, home, money, or relationship, you are to look at the big picture.

Before entering into this meditation, you should be clear on what that big picture is, and if you've done the various exercises described previously, you should at least have a starting point

Before you begin this meditation, you should definitely have a good idea of the desire you want to work on. You should have most of the details worked out on paper. These details should include the full experience of your desire. How you will see it . . . hear it . . . feel it . . . and even taste and smell it, if appropriate.

I recommend that you record yourself reading this meditation so you can conveniently listen to it at any time. I give instructions on when to pause in your reading. Just a nice, slow, comfortable pace will do the trick!

This meditation is designed to *fully* put you into the experience of the reality of your vision *now.* The more time you spend with this vision, the quicker you will realize it. You will experience your vision on all sensory levels, including emotion. Before you begin this meditation, you should have at least some vision of these things. That is really important. What you create should be your idea of absolute perfection. It is not harder to create "perfection" than it is to create something that makes your life miserable! So go with perfection and boundless happiness!

Please be sure to give yourself enough time to go through the meditation in its entirety. Make certain that you will not be disturbed and that you are as comfortable as possible. Everything about this experience should be joyous! You do not want to be thinking about anything else or having any stray worries running in the background. The conditions need to be right, because this meditation is extremely powerful.

Getting into a routine would be ideal. Set aside a block of forty-five minutes each day just for creating your reality in this way. It will be an incredibly profitable investment in time. When you are on a schedule, others will respect that time-slot, and you can be assured that you will have the right environment.

This meditation uses a lot of visual imagery. I understand that not everyone possesses the ability to visualize clearly. I do believe, however, that cultivating this ability is important. Still, if the images do not come, try this: simply *pretend* that you see the images. In other words, imagine what it would be like to see the images. Although you may doubt that something like this can work, the ability to see your imagination visually might just sneak up on you. In any case, do not worry if you cannot yet create clear pictures. Just immerse yourself in the thoughts and feelings of your desire.

The idea is to put yourself among the images you're creating, rather than "viewing" them as if you were watching them on television.

Unlike other meditations, this is not one that you "bring yourself out of" at the end. There are no statements like, "You will find yourself back in your chair . . . " or anything that would suggest that your current reality is any more real than the one you are creating in the meditation! You will be exactly where you should be in your experience when you are ready to end the meditation. A logical place is when the recording ends, but of course, you are welcome to stay in the reality you have created as long as possible!

So if you are ready, get comfortable, get excited about your desire, and let's make some major adjustments to your vibrational state!

Record the following:

Begin by shifting your awareness to your breathing. Your breaths should be full and natural, and you should have your attention simply on your breath. If your mind should wander, just ease your attention back to your breath. We are going to do this for a few minutes to enter a relaxing state. Just keep a natural cycle of cleansing oxygen circulating through your body. Pay particular attention to the space between your breaths . . . the point where the inhale becomes the exhale . . . and the exhale becomes the inhale.

Just continue to put your attention on your breathing.

As you lie here, turn your attention to what it feels like physically to exist in your current form. Experience, from head to toe, what it feels like to be in the physical at this moment.

Try to imagine yourself as a glowing form of Energy. This Energy is taking the form of your body, but only because you are currently creating it that way. Now, imagine your body disintegrating into the atomic particles of which it is composed. It feels something like a buzzing, or a vibration throughout your being . . . almost electric!

The buzz of this Energy gives you a feeling of lightness and freedom. You realize that you are Energy with Infinite possibilities of experience, which are determined completely by your thoughts . . . which interpret this sea of Energy all around you into what you perceive to be your reality. Imagine that by simply using your imagination, you can interpret this Energy in any way you'd like to create images, sounds, smells, and other sensory sensations.

Think for a moment about the vision you have created for yourself. As you do, pictures will naturally begin to form in your mind's eye.

Bring these images into focus in full 3D as if you are there right now. Take the time to fully observe as many details as you possibly can. You are experiencing your vision as a reality. Begin to allow the emotions of excitement and gratitude to come forth as you continue to surround yourself with the details of your vision.

You see, in bright colors, this new reality you have created simply by shifting your awareness. You are there. It is all around you.

Spend a moment just really sharpening and enhancing that image.

Pause.

Choose something in this reality to touch. Touch something and feel the characteristics of its surface. Really experience its texture.

Feel its temperature . . . cool? Warm? Touch as many things as you possibly can that represent the realization of your vision and really experience the sensation of physical contact.

Pause.

Hear any sounds associated with the experience of your vision now fulfilled. They are all around you, now! You are now seeing, feeling, and hearing the vision and reality.

What about smells? Think of any smells that you naturally associate with this vision. Fill your being with any aroma you can detect and, as you do, take in a deep breath and let it out slowly and fully.

Take another breath and again bring the reality of your experience into your being . . . hold it there a moment, allowing your reality to fully permeate you. Then exhale slowly and fully.

If there are any tastes associated with this desire, add these to your experience. Bring in the flavor of this experience if at all possible. You want to wake up every sensory receptor in your body and allow it to experience your new reality fully and completely!

Finally, check in with your emotions. Amplify the emotions you are feeling now that you have realized this desire. Make the emotions bigger and grander! More excited and joyous!

And now, send out the Energy of extreme gratitude that your vision has become your reality so completely and perfectly. Give thanks, and give more thanks, and feel that Energy of gratitude flow out of your being and into the rest of the Universe as energetic reciprocation for the ability to so effortlessly create your experience of reality.

Spend as much time as you want to in this vision. Continue to live the full sensory experience of your desire fulfilled. Fully enjoy the knowledge that you have created a new and ultimately fulfilling reality that is yours to step into now.

No matter which process you use to visualize, it's a good exercise to go through the process of creating or refining the vision, continuing your visualization exercises to generate the feelings associated with that vision, and then noticing and eliminating resistance as it shows itself. Then use that feedback to either refine your vision to be more in alignment with who you truly want to be, or to continue to eliminate resistance that is blocking you from experiencing what you're very clear you *do* want.

Just keep going through the process until you have a vision that inspires you every time you read, write, or think about it. You will get to a point where you experience little if any emotional or intellectual resistance in the process. When you accomplish that, you've taken the most important and powerful step there is.

So much time is wasted by people on the "self-help" track because they don't take the time on the front end to get really clear on what they want their lives to be. Instead, they set their attention on the problems that they're trying to solve by going through libraries of self-help material.

Don't get me wrong. There is absolutely great self-help education available. But there's a vast difference between being someone who uses self-help material to set themselves into action, and being a person who immerses themselves in self-help material on which they take no action.

That may seem silly, but it's what people do. When you *become* a "person who is working on him or herself," then that is who you will always be until you decide to step powerfully into *being who you truly desire to be.*

When visualization becomes a regular practice, you begin to make significant changes in your energetic vibration, and the Universe will respond. Much of that response will come in the form of what I call "intuitive nudges." You will begin to receive signals from the Universe in the form of your intuition providing guidance. Therefore it's important to understand how to recognize your intuition, and even more importantly, how to act on it.

Hearing Your Intuition

Because I put so much emphasis on following your intuition as you walk your path, I'm often asked how one knows if a thought that occurs to them during this walk is intuition, or whether it's some kind of resistance that is actually working against them.

Intuition is a natural part of being human, but it's a power that I believe lies all but dormant in most of us—and when we do get a message through our intuition, we've been given virtually no training in how to recognize it, so we ignore it or write it off as some random crazy thought.

As a result, learning to recognize your intuition can take some practice—some trial and error.

Over time, you'll begin to get a very distinct sense when a message is coming from your intuition and when it's resistance. There are very different energies associated with each, but it can take some time and experience with tuning in to your body's Energy system before you will be able to recognize the differences.

One thing is certain. When you start down your path as we instruct—keeping your vision at the forefront of your consciousness and releasing any resistance that shows up—you *will* start to receive messages in the form of intuition.

As such, if you're new to this whole "intuition" conversation, you should be on the lookout for thoughts or messages that are outside the norm for you. When you get the notion to call a friend, pay attention to that. If certain words jump off a newspaper, notice that. If you are unexpectedly invited to go somewhere that isn't part of your usual routine, this could also be indicative of the Universe providing direction for you.

This is a good time to remember that your path will be laid out *for* you. You don't have to have it all planned out and know everything you're going to do in advance. Of course, if such a plan comes to you, that could also be an intuitive message, and you should certainly take action on it. Just don't get attached to it, as the plan may evolve once you get to a certain point.

If you're going to trust the Universe/your intuition, it is best to do it consistently, even when—and sometimes especially when—it makes no logical sense to do so in the context of your vision.

My life changed when I finally gave up trying to make sense of absolutely everything before I'd make a move. There are still areas in my life where I tend to want all the answers before I act, but I'm always much more satisfied in the end with endeavors that were born out of true inspiration, and where I'm guided intuitively step by step through the process, even if I don't know for sure what the next step is going to be.

Be yourself in all that you do, and your intuition will be there to serve you in wonderful ways.

Start paying attention to the thoughts and ideas that occur to you, and if it feels right (or at least doesn't feel wrong,) take some action on that idea and just see how things unfold. Don't attach to anything specific. Don't try to guess what will happen.

Just be in the moment. Because walking your path is nothing more than a series of *now* moments. The goal is to make each one a beautiful experience.

Common Forms of Resistance

As human beings playing out in the world, we do not live isolated lives. Because we are up to things in the world, we're *out there*—with other people, in an infinite number of circumstances where many events occur as random and without explanation.

We've grown up in this world cultivating a system of beliefs that may or may not serve us. We've learned to judge people and situations, often far too prematurely. And all of these beliefs and the learning that we've done is stored away in our memories. But there is also Energy—just like everything else in the Universe.

Those beliefs that go against what we are trying to attract have a very strong Energy of their own.

These beliefs can be many years running, and contrast strongly to the new beliefs that you are trying to cultivate with regard to living a boundless life.

Without tending, these "rogue Energies" will continue to have an impact on your overall vibrational state. Regardless of how many times you affirm something in the positive, if your subconscious mind believes the opposite and that belief evokes an emotional response, then your vibration will be tainted, and thus unable to fully resonate in alignment with your ultimate vision.

Thus, we call it "resistance" because it is literally resisting what you say you want.

Let's take a quick look at a few ways resistance shows up:

Negative Self-Talk

These are all the voices in your head from your past that have manifested into rogue Energy systems that are a part of who you are. These systems are in a state of imbalance that result in our experience of negative feelings and poor physical health.

Learning to release, therefore, has tremendous benefits all the way around.

Some common voices you might here as you start down the path:

"I can't do that."

"It's not my fault, but . . . "

"I can't figure it out . . . "

"I'm not smart enough."

"I don't deserve this."

"This isn't happening fast enough."

"I'm wasting my time. This will never work."

People

Resistance shows up as people all the time.

Remember that up to this point in your life, you have attracted everyone appropriately. Friends, co-workers, and yes—even family. You are in vibrational resonance with all of these people to some extent, whether you "enjoy" them all or not.

Every person in your life is somehow a physical expression of some aspect of yourself. How do we know this?

It's virtually impossible to look at someone and not make some level of judgment about them. I don't mean that you judge them deeply or harshly—good or bad. I'm simply acknowledging that your brain has some kind of response to everything it experiences, and people are no exception.

These judgments could be anything from "tall," "skinny," "heavy," to slightly deeper things like "he looks nice," "she looks like a jerk," "anyone who dresses like that is obviously . . . "

Whatever the level of judgment, it speaks more of ourselves than of the person we're judging. So if you react negatively to a person, it is you that is at cause for the negativity. Regardless of what the other person is doing or "being" that is annoying to you, your annoyance is born in you, not the other person. That annoyance gives you some insight into areas of resistance you may not even know you have.

Why does that person annoy you? What buttons do they push? Are there specific memories that you can conjure up that evoke a similar emotional response?

The point is, the root of the negativity lies in patterns of resistance in *you* that are actively running, and they are shaping your vibration. This is how you attract these annoying people even though you don't want to. You are a vibrational match to them for some reason, and you're giving up a lot of your personal Energy through your annoyance.

If you want to attract a different kind of person, you have to change what you are vibrating, and do some release work in certain areas. The great news is that this is what this journey is all about! Changing your vibration through walking your own path will cause a change in who you surround yourself with.

But herein lies a challenge.

Simply because you have chosen to live more authentically and powerfully inside of who you are doesn't mean that everyone around you will see the same for you.

Remember, these people are in your life because you were, up to this point, a vibrational match for them. Now you're changing who you are in a significant way. You're going through a true energetic transformation.

What you're "putting out there" now may *not* resonate with the people in your life, and what's going to show up is *their stuff.*

Anytime a person tells you what isn't possible for you, keep firmly in mind that this is *their stuff.* They are speaking *their* truth, most likely about what *they* see as possible or not for *themselves.* They're just directing it at you.

If these are people close to us, it is going to be very easy for us to be "triggered" by familiar emotional patterns or behavioral patterns that quickly return us to our own familiar emotional responses.

Admittedly, it is not always easy to get through this time of transition. This is why it is so important to know that the vision you've created for yourself leads to great rewards, unlike anything you've experienced before. The vision must be able to pull you through the most difficult of times, and this will be much easier for you when you've mastered a good releasing technique.

When people are your obstacle, it is often because you are concerned about what they will think about you should you suddenly take a new direction in life.

At that point you have to ask yourself the all-important question:

Whose life am I living?

Are you living *your* life, or are you living a version of your life that you hope will please everyone else?

The honest answer to that question is important if you're truly going to walk your own path.

It is easy to get concerned over the fear associated with relationships transforming significantly or falling away completely, but that concern is also simply a choice we are making. Many of us have been taught that the ending of a relationship is something to be mourned. Instead, we can celebrate every moment of every relationship for what it meant to us. When the time comes to move on, we can do so with no hurt and no sadness, trusting that all was for the greater good, and that perhaps if appropriate, our paths will cross again.

Alas, we're not wired like that for the most part. We get attached to our relationships, even if we're clear that they are not serving us at all.

Indeed, it takes tremendous commitment to yourself to move through the "people obstacles" related to committing to living your vision, and it's mostly because of how we've been conditioned to emotionally respond in relationship-oriented situations.

Another way we perceive people as obstacles is as literal obstructions: "He/she won't let me." or "He/she is preventing me from doing it."

In these cases, you have chosen to give up your personal power to someone else for some reason. The reasons could be infinite. And if you're using this as a reason, you probably rationalize doing so very well. After all, you can probably point to situation after situation where he/she was a block to your progress. What you're *not* seeing is that you have attracted that person because you yourself have resistance to actually "doing it" (whatever it is), and you have literally manifested a person who will tell you not to, or make it seem like you can't.

Until you eliminate your own resistance to doing what you truly want, these people will always show up in your life in some form in a way that will give you a reason to stop. The benefit is that you get to blame someone else, absolving yourself of responsibility.

The problem with blaming someone else, of course, is that it again takes away all your power, and leaves you with no options whatsoever.

An infinite number of options are available to you if you allow them in. When you can take responsibility for the obstacles that show up simply by acknowledging that somehow you are in vibrational resonance with them, then you have the power to consciously choose to resonate with something else. This might be a whole new set of people who come into your life to fully support you in your vision. At the same time that you are bringing these people into your life, you are allowing *them* to express who they truly are as well. The value of the combined group can create more change in the world than you can imagine . . . simply because *you* started down your path.

Life Occurs

Situations in life are exactly like people, in that whatever situation you're in, you're in it because somehow you're in vibrational alignment with it.

I understand that if you're in a "bad situation," you don't want to take responsibility for it on any level, and may very well be offended by the very idea that you should own up to it.

However, once you understand and accept the very simple premise of the Law of Attraction that we attract into our experience those things with which we're in vibrational resonance, you will eventually be able to see that nothing is going to "break" that law. If you're not in resonance with something, it can't become a part of your experience. Resistance would simply push it away.

So the question becomes, "Okay, how did I get into vibrational resonance with (whatever bad thing happened)?"

It sure would be great if I could tell you specifically how and why something showed up in your life, but the fact is that it could be countless things. You could have deep beliefs that you don't even know about. You might watch a lot of news and hear about all kinds of horrific things around the world. When you do that, if you're not careful, you integrate those events as "things that can occur." It's very subtle, but everything you put into your brain has an impact. It shapes how you think—the lens through which you see the world.

As you look through that lens, you're going to have emotional responses to what you see. And those responses will be a result of all the input you've taken in ever since you were a thinking human being. What you've been told by parents, teachers, preachers, the media, the government, and your friends.

Add to that all you've read, experienced, and thought about. And all of those nuances blend together to create your overall vibration and thus what is possible in your life—whether you think consciously about it or not.

There's a lot going on with us vibrationally that we never think about, but that is having a very significant impact on our experience of life.

This is the essence of "why bad things happen to good people." It has nothing to do with them being at "fault," and we're not suggesting that they somehow intentionally attracted the bad event. Although this isn't necessarily a comfort to many people, the answer to the question as to why bad things happen to good people is that the good people were *somehow*—on some level—in vibrational alignment with the event.

It's simply not always going to make sense to us from our limited perspective.

Here's something else to consider. All those events we're interpreting as bad? Remember we're *choosing* to feel that way. Right or wrong, that decision is a choice we make because of social conditioning.

I say all this to simply make the important point that you ultimately *choose* your emotional state. And since your emotional state has direct impact on your vibration and what you can attract, it will serve you tremendously to learn to work with your emotions, rather than be at the mercy of them.

Now that you're learning new ways to release resistance, you will be able to uncover some of that hidden stuff and be free from it, potentially forever.

The Power of Gratitude

Gratitude is truly a powerful force. And like any emotion, gratitude is an Energy that attracts Energy with which it resonates.

In other words, when you are feeling gratitude, you are attracting more things to be grateful for.

Also, gratitude is just a plain good feeling. Think about how you feel when you're *truly* grateful for something. It's a very pleasant feeling, and one that can actually be sustained with practice.

It's easy to get distracted by our lives and all of our interpretations, and in the process to totally take for granted all the little miracles that surround us. Simple things like running water . . . the ability to breathe . . . the fact that you're able to read this. All of these "little things" can still create a powerful abundance magnet for you if you take the time to experience a genuine feeling of gratitude for anything and everything you can think of.

I'm certainly not saying that's what you should consciously do all day, but the more habitually you can notice, acknowledge, and emotionally appreciate your everyday "ordinary" life, the more extraordinary you're allowing it to come.

As you begin your journey down your path, little things are going to start to occur as you begin to powerfully attract the situations that are going to lead you where you want to go. Showing gratitude for these things—even the seemingly insignificant ones—will speed up the attraction of those to follow.

I highly recommend that you intentionally set aside time each day to keep a Gratitude Journal. This process is designed to get you in the habit of acknowledging all things—big and small—that you have to be grateful for.

Like all writing exercises described in books like this one, I understand that there will be those people who won't ever write a word in their Gratitude Journal. They try to remember to take note of things to be grateful for, but feel that the writing is an unnecessary step. I totally understand that mindset, as I am one of those people to a large degree.

However, if you're looking to make major changes in your life, you have to be willing to try things that you've never done before. After all, doing things the same way year after year is what perpetuates the very situations you're trying to change. I'm inviting you to "try on" being a person who is willing to do the work, however "unnecessary" it may seem. Keeping a Gratitude Journal is a great place to start your new practice.

Sometimes our situations seem so dire that we honestly feel like we have nothing to be grateful for. However, if you were to lose everything you have—everything—you would begin to get a true appreciation for the smallest things in your life. I imagine that were you to have a conversation with someone who has spent significant time in prison about gratitude for what they had on the outside, they would never stop talking.

Remember, the Universe doesn't think in terms of big and small. If you have a feeling of gratitude for a small thing in your life and can generate that feeling genuinely, the Universe responds the same way it does when you feel gratitude for the big things, and that's by bringing you more to be grateful for—big and small.

If you insist on clinging to your story that you have nothing to be grateful for, or very little, then the Universe will respond appropriately in that situation as well, perpetuating that reality for you.

It's your choice.

Putting It All Together

You have your vision.

You have a release technique.

You are learning to recognize and act on your intuition.

You understand the role of gratitude and how key it is.

This process will evolve into a way of being for you. These simple steps won't be something you're taking on as part of a "program," but a way of living your life exactly as you want it to be lived. It will become as natural as breathing.

Here's how to start:

1. At the beginning of every day, spend no less than five to ten minutes sitting inside your vision either through meditation or

some other way. Pay attention to what negative thoughts or feelings come up and do your release technique on them until the emotional charge is absent or greatly reduced. Some issues may take several sessions, or even some expert guidance.

2. End each meditative session with an invitation for the Universe to show you the next step in your journey.
3. Be tuned in to your intuition. Don't over-evaluate ideas as they pop into your head. If you're in a place to take any action at all on those ideas, do it. Sometimes the Universe provides "time-sensitive" opportunities.
4. Make it a point to feel true gratitude for whatever you have in your life to be at all thankful for, particularly with regards to even the slightest progress in your vision.
5. Hold your vision, act on your intuition, feel gratitude, release resistance. Repeat. Repeat. Repeat.

Those five steps are all it boils down to. That's all you have to do to walk your path and realize your vision . . . because when you do those things, the way opens up in front of you effortlessly. There is hardly any question as to what to do next as you learn to trust your intuition more and more, and maintain being in "the flow."

So that's it. I know it seems so simple when you boil it down, but now you should have a richer understanding of why this approach works, and you've been given the tools you need to move through stopping points like never before.

I urge you to not wait another minute.

Chapter 6

THE ANSWERS TO THE QUESTIONS YOU WILL HAVE

Once you start putting all that you've learned here into regular practice, you're no doubt going to have circumstances arise that we haven't covered.

Over the past decade, I've fielded literally thousands of questions on the topic of creating your life by design. This section addresses many of the questions you're liable to have, and although some of the information may seem repetitive, that is actually by design. This section can be thought of as a reference guide that you can refer to when these issues do show up for you. I'll review any pertinent principles so that you aren't expected to remember all the details in this book to be able to get the full value from whichever section you're reading.

If you're reading this the first time through, the repetition of certain fundamentals in the context of real-world scenarios should help to embed this information even deeper before you go out into the world and step into action on all that you've learned!

The Most Important Value You Can Give

If we want to receive anything in our lives—and that can be money, relationships, or just "stuff"—we have to provide value to the Universe. We do that by fully contributing what we have to give, by being who we truly are.

What we do during the bulk of the day and how we feel about it plays a large part in our vibrational state. Remember, the hour or so per day that we spend doing our visualization exercises is only a small portion of our waking life. If we are not very conscious about all this, especially at first, it will be the thoughts and feelings that we're having when we're not visualizing that dictate what comes into our lives.

It stands to reason, then, that if you are working at a job that is unsatisfying, or if you are otherwise unhappy with the occupation that takes up eight-plus hours of your day, that is a lot of time to be vibrating at a low or negative frequency.

If your inspired vision gets checked at the door of your workplace, then you are really sending the Universe mixed signals about what you perceive the reality of your life to be.

Let's assume that you wake up in the morning and spend time envisioning your perfect life. You get into the feeling and shift your vibration in a way that will accelerate the fulfillment of those desires. *Then* you think, "Okay, back to the real world. Gotta go to work." For the next ten hours, your thoughts are mired in a wholly unsatisfying pattern of thought that simply works to attract more of the same.

How much of your true value are you really contributing when so little of the "real you" is in your work? Not much! The amount of value that comes back to you in the form of a true feeling of abundance, joy, and prosperity will most likely not be has much as you'd hoped, despite the hours of labor you are putting in.

The hours are not the value. Value is not gauged by how hard you work. Value comes from answering this question: What is your contribution to the Universe? This is a more accurate assessment of value, because the quality of your "contribution," or your Energy, will improve as you live the life you truly desire to live, instead of the one you have been living by default without any real choice based in passion.

Perhaps you're thinking, "I *have* to go to work, though! Until this "attraction" stuff starts working for me, I have to pay the bills somehow! I can't wait around for the Universe to deliver. I need money now!"

This type of "flip-flop" thinking can be directly attributed to our friend the Ego. It is just so easy to listen to its logic sometimes. After all, there *are* bills that are due, and your bank account might not have the money to cover them.

What perpetuates your situation is the *emotion* associated with the statement, "I have got to pay my bills!" Here's the harsh reality: The Universe isn't looking out for your best interests. That's *your* job. The Universe delivers precisely in alignment with your vibration, whether it's a vibration you're putting out consciously or not.

So what is the obvious fix to this "job" thing? Well, it is simple. Find out what you love to do, and do that. The obvious objection comes, *"I'd love to, but it will not pay the bills,"* which makes that defensive excuse completely true for whoever says it—there is generally a lot of emotion around a statement like that, and it vibrates "lack" like crazy.

I know this from personal experience.

But here is what was true for me. Look closely at this: When I first was out there trying to make a living at what I "loved to do," it immediately became a *job*. Something felt "at stake." There was a "do or die" about it. Some of the passion and joy of the activities (and I tried several) was sucked right out, because I suddenly *needed* to make money with it.

What is the effect on your vibration when you engage in this kind of thinking? It plummets. You are now vibrating with stress, fear, and worry.

In your previous attempts to live your dream, you might have had fun . . . but were you also aware of the Law of Attraction? Did you have a clear vision of the life you truly wanted to design? Or were you going through your day-to-day life, doing what you loved but with no clear direction, or with a nagging feeling in the back of your mind that your life might not pan out exactly as you'd hoped?

Really consider this carefully. The answer to why your attempt at making a living from your passions did not work in the past lies in the honest answers to these questions. If you had no clear vision, then raising your vibrations by doing what you loved only served to bring you more of whatever it is you were vibrating or thinking about. If you were not creating a future vision, then your thoughts were probably just on your day-to-day activities, so you remained where you were. When you did not see "progress" it is because you really did not define (and generate positive emotion around) what progress actually *was made* or how it could be measured. As a result, your Ego started to second-guess your decision to "do what you loved" for a living.

The moment that happened, you began your descent. Because you were not consciously aware that you should have reversed that thinking immediately, you just followed this counter-productive thought process downward, which resulted in the manifestation of negative situations.

Then you made the conclusion, "Well, I tried it and I failed." And you started looking for a new "real job" . . . when that was not necessarily your only option, and certainly not the way to attract wealth, particularly if you simply settled for a job that did not fulfill you.

All of this underlines the theme of this book, which is to be who you truly are. Do what you are *meant* to do without worry or apology. As a result, your vibration will naturally rise and your predominant thoughts, desires, and intentions will come to you more readily. Why? Because when you are being fully and completely who you truly are, contributing your natural, unique gifts to the world and loving virtually every moment of your life, you will put out vibrations in precise alignment with what you want to experience in your life, and in the process you will contribute maximum value to the Universe as a whole! The reward for that is your ability to live whatever life you want.

Pretty nice reward, I'd say.

Understand that You Deserve It

For a person to be able to manifest anything into their lives, they need to believe that they deserve it. To really understand this, we need to review the most simple truths about the nature of our existence.

At a most basic level, we are a system of Energy that "manifests" itself into cells, tissue, organs, and so on—into the form of a human being. With all these cells, tissues, and organs, *we are given the ability to experience a wide range of other Energy frequencies around us.*

We experience these frequencies as things "outside" of us—like chairs, houses, money, other people, etc., but they are not *outside* us as much as they are a *part* of us. We experience the illusion of separateness, because the frequency at which our Energy is vibrating is magnetically attracting Energy vibrating at a resonant frequency. We bring into our experience those things that we attract to us.

And how do we attract? By now, you know it is through the power of our thoughts and emotions—that we actually generate magnetic Energy. We have been given the incredible gifts of *imagination* and emotion. Emotions allow us to experience our reality in ways that many other configurations of Energy, such as a table, cannot.

We can feel joy, exuberance, and passion! And doing so will attract Energy to us in various forms that will cause us to feel more of those feelings. This Energy can be in the form of other people, things, or any other experiences that we desire!

On the other hand, we can choose to feel fear, pain, sadness, guilt, or jealousy, and thus attract Energy that manifests an environment that will sustain *these* feelings. It all begins with our choice, but there are many facets to our choice!

On the surface, our choices seem so simple:

"I want a new car. I choose that Mercedes, right there."

Below that surface description of our desire, there are many other conversations going on, such as:

"I do not have enough money," or "I do not really *need* it, I guess," or the one that most people do not even know they have: "I do not *deserve* that car."

All of these responses are false. You learned them over the course of your life, simply because you did not know any better. Somewhere along the line, you were exposed to Energy systems, perhaps in the form of parents, friends, or your physical environment, which instilled these thoughts as beliefs. Remember, the truth is that you are a magnificent configuration of Energy that has the ability to manifest into its experience—*your* experience—whatever you desire. But your desire has to include your *allowance* of its fulfillment. Those thoughts like, "I can't afford it" and more importantly, "I do not deserve it" are exactly what is stopping you from that fulfillment.

There are few thoughts more universally prohibitive than "I do not deserve it." If your foundational belief and feelings are that you do not deserve something, then none of your other thoughts will override such a core belief.

If you are truly vibrating that you do not deserve something, then that something cannot be attracted to you, at least not for any extended period of time.

On the other hand, if you *do* feel that you deserve something, it is much easier for you to allow it to flow into your life.

There is an important distinction that needs to be made here. Truly feeling you deserve something by divine inheritance is much different than taking a position that you *think* you deserve something because you did this or that nice thing and that somebody somewhere ought to give you what's coming to you. This thought process is based on a lack mentality, or one of earth-level "fairness."

Deserving, as we are talking about it, has nothing to do with thinking you should have something because you do great things and you should be compensated. For example, you do not deserve what you want because you are a good person or because you give to charity or because you have worked your fingers to the bone for decades and the time has come for the payoff.

You deserve what you want simply because it is the part of the design of the Universe that you experience your desires.

Your desires are a gift to you. They tell you your purpose. They tell you precisely what is intended in your life. It is only our limited thinking that prohibits us from immediately experiencing those things. We have learned that we must "work for them" or "earn them," when the truth is, "Ask, and you shall receive."

We, as humans, have attached this judgmental meaning to the word "deserve." We have decided that someone must validate us or that we must validate ourselves based on things we do, how successful we are, how hard we work, or a countless number of other man-made metrics by which we gauge our worth.

We have allowed our memories, beliefs, thoughts, and emotions to define who we think we are. We are truly more than all of those things. They simply determine our experience, and all of those are flexible. They are thoughts that you are having in this present moment. They may occur to you as the "past," or what you believe your future will be, but in actuality, they are simply how you are choosing to interpret the sum total of your experience of the Universe in this moment. Therefore, it is *in this moment* that you can change everything.

You have to start with knowing that you deserve what you want. When you do, there is very little (aside from other areas of resistance you might be dealing with) stopping you from having it.

On the surface, you might not even be aware that you have any issues with "deserving," but what I can assure you is that if there is something you want in your life that you do not yet have—and particularly if you have wanted it for a long time—and even *more* particularly if you have been working with the Law of Attraction to get it—it is most likely because at some level you feel you do not truly deserve it—at least not right now.

Perhaps we feel more deserving of things if we work a little longer . . . or if we are a little nicer to people. Then, we feel we *deserve* what we want, and only then do we allow it into our experience, through a vibration that fully resonates with what we desire.

This is a hidden issue for many people. When we get started with the Law of Attraction, we gain the understanding that we need to know what we want, that we need to generate positive emotion around it, and that we need to release resistance around it. Issues with deserving are just another form of resistance, which you now have the tools to eliminate.

By the way, there is a difference between believing you deserve something "someday" and believing that you deserve it *right now.* You *do* deserve it now. It is up to *you* to determine when you will actually allow it into your life.

Here is a process that will help you to identify areas within yourself where you may be feeling undeserving or challenged by "hidden" blockages that prevent your desires from being fulfilled.

Think of one of your most passionate desires, one of the big ones that perhaps you have been thinking about for some time.

Close your eyes and fully visualize and get into the feeling of your desire fulfilled. What would it *mean* if, when you opened your eyes, the desire had manifested right in front of you? Think about what your honest reaction would be.

Let's say it was a car. You close your eyes, visualize the car, feel what it would be like to be in that car driving along the open road, smelling the leather of the seats—all that stuff. Then you open your eyes and your car is sitting there right in front of you.

You would probably freak out, wouldn't you? You would most likely be so incredibly frightened that you would run screaming! I mean, think about it. Could you open your eyes, see a car before you that appeared out of thin air, and just sit calmly, feel wonderful, and thank the Universe for bringing your desire to you?

Doubtful. Why is that?

Probably because it is just too big! What defines something as "big" or "small" as it relates to a desire? It is determined by just how far out of your comfort zone it is, how far this item is outside what you consider to be your current parameters of reality.

You might feel as though you deserve the car, but do you feel that you deserve the ability to manifest it instantaneously? Probably not. That comes from simply not understanding the true reason you are here. If it is any consolation, just about nobody fully allows the true power that they have at their disposal. There are just far too many years and lifetimes of having "learned" our limitations.

- Do you feel you deserve good health now?
- Do you feel you deserve a lean body now?
- Do you feel you deserve abundance now?
- Do you feel you deserve a happy marriage now?

The wording of these questions is important, because it is not an issue of whether or not you actually *do* deserve something . . . because you most definitely do. You deserve anything and everything you desire.

You are this miracle of Creation for the express purpose of using this unique gift called imagination to bring forth your desires into reality. Anything that stops you from feeling that you deserve your desires is based on false information, which can be unlearned. Once you do unlearn it, watch out! You will turn into a manifestation machine!

Next time anything at all happens to you that you do not enjoy, ask yourself if you truly believe that you deserve a *better* situation. However, you must understand that all of your circumstances are brought to you through the Law of Attraction. You are literally vibrating a frequency that has brought this and all other circumstances to you.

You do not have to believe it. Your belief in any of this has no effect on how the Law works. It will, however, have an effect on how the Law *occurs* for you.

Here is an easy way to gauge how "deserving" you truly feel at the deepest and most important levels:

Look around you. What do you see?

Whatever you are looking at is an indicator of what you feel you deserve. Nothing more and nothing less.

Now, let me explain that.

"Deserving," the way most humans think about it, is an intellectual process of sorts. They figure that given everything they have said and done throughout their lives, they have "earned" (or they "deserve") to have a certain experience. They "deserve" to have a house that is X size, a car that costs X amount of dollars, or a marriage that is X happy.

On the outside, they might look at their environment and complain, "I can't believe this! I deserve so much more than this! This is not fair."

The tricky part to understand is that those statements are not reflective of your *true* beliefs. They may be intellectually sound, however. That is, you may work much harder than you are being compensated for. You may treat people a lot nicer than they treat you. You may be loyal to a spouse who does not return that courtesy. Therefore, you figure that you "deserve" better and that some cosmic injustice is being done.

While all that may be so, there are two things that are also true:

First, you are having the experience you are having because, on some level, you are in vibrational resonance with it.

Secondly, the reason you are vibrating the way you are is that, at your deepest levels, you do not really feel you deserve any better (or worse) than you have right now. The reasons for that can run really deep and are the kinds of things that can be extracted through the releasing techniques described in this book.

However, none of that really matters, because it has no bearing whatsoever on whether or not you are deserving.

The proof that you deserve anything you desire is the fact that you exist.

Since most people do not understand that, they have created this limiting system of Energy within themselves that they label as "being deserving only if . . . " They literally hold themselves back from the exact experience they were put here to have.

This is something of an advanced concept, but to the extent that you can understand it, your manifesting skills will improve exponentially. When you truly know you deserve anything you want, you are well on your way to having it.

Your Desires Are Already Fulfilled

One of the ideas that is taught, mostly by the more metaphysically oriented Law of Attraction teachers, is the concept that each of us *already has* everything we desire, we just have to shift our awareness toward it.

This concept either requires a big fat leap of blind faith, or a much deeper understanding of quantum physics and the multidimensional nature of our Universe. I prefer the latter.

I know that a concept like that is difficult to believe. I mean, our current situations sometimes feel so real and so permanent that it is difficult to grasp that I idea that we can just "realize" something else. Our desire certainly does not seem to exist "here," so where *does* it exist?

It exists in our thoughts, and this should not be undervalued. We can see it in our mind's eye. If we do what we should when we have a desire for something, we also feel it with all of our senses and focus our imagination and attention on the emotion involved with having this desire fulfilled. When we do that, our desire has been brought into energetic existence and it is just waiting for us to bring it into a more tangible form. We have assembled the Energy that is now pure potential to be an experience in our life. The problem is that so many of us do not consider our thoughts to be "real," but simply nonexistent imaginary images in our brain.

The Energy that is your current experience of reality and the Energy of the "thought" of your desire are simply vibrating on two totally different frequencies for you. Shift the Energy of your current awareness to the "other" frequency, and you will become in resonance with it—it will become a part of your reality. Because we are not conscious of this, we just simply let our awareness follow the "easiest" path, based on its belief systems. We have programmed ourselves, or it has been programmed into us, to think and "do life" in this manner.

The fact is that we can and *should* reclaim conscious control over our awareness. This book has outlined all the steps you need to do that, and what is left is for you to take action. If you have gotten clear on your desires, done your visualizations, and have begun getting those intuitive nudges, but you haven't yet stepped into action, you are either dealing with resistance, or you just have not fully integrated the immense possibility that lies ahead when you begin to consciously create your life. All it takes is a little more control over the use of your imagination.

Imagination is our greatest tool of creation, and it is free for us to use at any time. If we do not use it, life will seem totally out of our control, and our circumstances may appear extremely grim—but that's simply because of what we believe. Remember, your Ego is going to "support" you in this reality of yours with all kinds of logical reasons why you cannot change your circumstances in an instant. Those are lies, even though they seem so easy to believe. That is why so many people believe in them.

To reiterate: you *do* have your desires now. They came into being the moment you imagined them. If they seem to exist only in the domain of your imagination, that's just because you are interpreting Energy in a certain way right now. You have the ability to change your interpretation by creating a "replacement" reality in your imagination. However, that is as far as many of us take it. We do not then "step in" to what we have created, because we have totally blocked out the knowledge that we know how to do that. All knowledge is ours if we claim it. We are just stuck in this loop of logic that tells us what is possible for us. In fact, it is all possible. Right now.

If finding the time to explore all this is an issue, start by taking five to ten minutes of time just to "be" with your desire. Bring it forth in your imagination and surround it with nothing but positive feelings and emotions. In your mind's eye, experience your desire on every sensory level—see it, hear it, touch it—and *in your vision*, think about how grateful you are to be experiencing the desire right now. To the extent that you commit yourself to this, your desire will absolutely come to you more quickly. As with all visualization exercises, this is the perfect opportunity to release whatever resistance appears as you do this.

The more you practice this, the more the Ego begins to accept the change. "Ego" is beginning to get the message, as you give it the experience of the positive feelings associated with your desire. Sooner or later, the Ego says, "Hey, this new thing feels so much better than this current thing we've got going. Let's live in the new thing."

Then your awareness will begin to shift. If you only *tease* your Ego with the experience of your desire, only taking time to visualize it as I described every now and then, the Ego will not know you are serious. It is going to cling to what is comfortable and "controllable" until it realizes that this new situation is going to make it even happier. I am not saying the Ego is in ultimate control, but when we first start with practicing these principles, it is one of the loudest voices we hear screaming, "It can't be done."

You are on a path to self-discovery. You are on your way to learning more about your purpose and what is possible for you and all of humanity. This book is just another step along your path. I believe that knowledge of the fact that it is *you* who creates your own experience is one of the most important realizations you will ever have. If you forget this ability, life can be a series of struggles and battles. It simply doesn't have to be that way.

Attracting Specific Things

When I first starting working intentionally with the Law of Attraction, my wife and I went to see a 1.7-million-dollar home that was for sale on a lake near our house.

Visiting this home was an incredible experience. Initially, I approached this visit as an exercise in raising my wealth consciousness, because at that time, 1.7 million dollars was a price range that had my Ego wanting to scream!

I wanted to put myself in a place that had no evidence of lack whatsoever and just *experience* it. It was a residence that I knew had a few of the features I was looking for in "the ultimate home."

Now, you need to know a few things. On my list of desires I had at the time, a house on the lake was at the top of the list. From there, I created details like:

- Every room wired for audio
- A computer in the kitchen for recipe access
- Heated tile floors
- Multiple showerheads
- A nice dock
- Deep water for swimming
- A media room

You get the idea. Before I even saw the house, I had very specific "visions," if you will, of the view of the water from various rooms. One vision in particular, was very clear. I was sitting in a chair in a long, hardwood floor room, a fireplace to my left, a wall of arched windows in front of me, with a view of the water. It was so vivid . . . I knew it was *the room.*

So you can imagine what went through my head when I walked into this house for the first time and saw, in the living room, the exact scene that I had been viewing in my imagination for months. I about fell over . . . and at the same time, I knew that this was totally right.

It continued from there. Every room had speakers for music. There was a heated tile floor in the bathroom, and nine showerheads. There was even a small refrigerator in the master bath. I did not create the refrigerator in my vision, but knowing me, I probably would have eventually!

The house had decks off every bedroom, perfect for entertaining and just as I'd imagined. I love decks . . . and this house has decks galore! There was a beautiful dock in a cove of deep water, a view of the marina off in the distance, and great sunsets. The house was built by a contractor for his personal use. He had intended to live in the home for the rest of his life, so you can imagine the quality and attention to detail that had gone into the construction.

There was even a computer in the kitchen.

What did this mean? I tried not to jump to the interpretation that this was necessarily *my* house . . . or that it was coming in the immediate future. It *could have* meant that, but at the time, I felt it was not for me to decide. Rather than get immediately attached to that house, I chose to follow my intuition, pay attention to my ideas, and keep the vision alive.

Seeing this house really added some power to this whole experience of "being wealthy." After touring the house, I had something very real and specific to focus my creative Energy on. The house was no longer just a collection of concepts in my head. I had seen it and touched it. I knew it existed physically. I just had to resist the urge to try to "figure out" how it was coming, if indeed that was the house that was to someday be ours.

Clearly, the Universe was in the process of delivering an experience in alignment with my vibration at the time. The "coincidences" of this experience were absolutely ridiculous. One would have to be totally blind, or at least very closed-minded, not to see that. I mean, it is almost as if the guy built this house according to the very spec sheet that I had just started creating a few months prior to actually stepping foot inside the home.

You may be wondering if we ever moved into that house.

We did not. As much as I loved the house, moving into a place that was so remote would have created family turmoil. My daughters were teenagers at the time, and my wife was involved with a tennis league that made her very happy. While I might have enjoyed living in the house itself, creating upset in my family was definitely *not* in alignment with the vibrations I was putting out with regards to a dream house.

As it turns out, we moved into another home. Though it was not on a lake, it did meet the essence of my list of desires. In other words, it was still a vibrational match for what I envisioned as my dream home.

Further, we later learned that the house on the lake had issues with mold that would have become a nightmare for us had we purchased it.

The point is, I used that house on the lake as something of a "touchstone" that I could bring forth in my imagination to generate the feelings associated with the joy of living in our next home. I was not attached to that home in particular, but instead basked in the feelings that thoughts of the home generated.

This is a key distinction.

All too often, people get attached to attracting a specific thing or person, when what is really important is the emotional essence of the object of desire.

I am often asked if one can use the Law of Attraction to attract a relationship with a specific individual. Often that individual is either currently showing no interest in the person asking the question, or is involved in another relationship. It is neither appropriate, nor will it work, to try to bring that person to you if it is not their will.

The key here however, is that it is not the *person* that you want, but the emotional experience you believe you will have by being with that person. If you want to use a specific person as a model for what you want, that is fine as long as you don't get so attached to that person that you miss all the opportunities that come your way as a result of being in that vibration of attracting the perfect person for you.

The message here for you is to dream big and dream specifically, but use the specificity to really fine-tune what you're putting out there energetically in terms of a vibration, rather than being attached to a particular outcome. My "dream house" showed up in our lives almost immediately after I began to meditate on what I wanted our ideal home to be, and yet it was a totally different house that ultimately fulfilled that dream.

Play with "being" wealthy. Shop for a home, a car, or *something* that connects you with the feeling of wealth. It's even more effective than just simply visualizing in your mind, and it is just fun to do!

I'll add that if you are going to do this exercise to feel what it's like to experience "expensive" things, *do not think about the money.* Shop as if paying for it is not even the issue. Go find what excites you! That does *not* mean that you should spend a bunch of money if money is not currently a part of your experience, particularly if you are one who stresses over debt. Simply think about what you are going to end up with when you have it.

Further, when you think about money, you can get caught up in the "how" of the process and focus on trying to figure out ways the money will come, which is not your job. Just follow the signs and have the most fun possible.

This is a good point to talk about the "This, or something better for the good of all concerned" addendum you might want to place at the end of your statements of desire. For example, if I had been too attached to this particular lake house, I would have run the risk of missing the opportunity to snag the house we got.

You want to remain detached until the desire is ultimately fulfilled. That does not mean "do nothing." You *will* most likely be taking action, but take action as the Universe leads you and don't try to forge the path yourself with intellectual thinking. Now, if "planning it all out" feels totally natural, freeing, and just "right" to do, then perhaps that is your path—but if you have any stress or worry around creating a plan, that is not what you need to be doing.

So write, visualize, and go out and play in the real world, and have a blast doing it. When you do, you can be sure that the items on which you put your quality attention are on their way.

Who Wants to "Be" a Millionaire?

You might be thinking "Me!" in answer to that question . . . but I will bet that you are really thinking, "I want to have a million dollars." For the purposes of this conversation, these are not the same thing, though it certainly seems like they are at first. Doesn't the word "millionaire" imply that you have a million dollars?

Yes, that is exactly what it does. It implies you have a million dollars. I am sure there are people who call themselves millionaires who often have *more* than a million dollars in the bank and sometimes have *LESS*. The distinction is this: Who they *are*—who they are *being*—is a millionaire. They will most likely always be a millionaire, if they truly have developed the mindset of a millionaire and are thus naturally attracting wealth through the Law of Attraction.

The fact is, what you're probably really thinking is that you'd like for money to never be an issue for you. Many believe that there is something magical about a million dollars—as if that number automatically solves all problems and makes dreams come true. I invite you to focus more on the *feeling* that you believe having a million dollars will give you than on the actual number. From this point, let's refer to a millionaire as someone who has taken on the mindset of a person who feels financially free.

Let me share some insight on the feelings you might want to try to integrate into your everyday way of being.

A *true* millionaire does not have to worry about losing everything. "Millionaire" has become a state of mind for them, not a number in a bank account. The feeling of being a millionaire or someone who will always have plenty of money is unique. When I first started "trying it on," as I am going to suggest *you* do, it was a very powerful feeling. The experience was not in terms of power over anything, but I felt a very significant surge through my being.

For seconds at a time, I would cross over into a true millionaire mindset and every worry in my life, small and large, that had *anything* to do with money or the lack thereof, completely vanished. The feeling is indescribable. "Wealth" suddenly permeated all aspects of my being, and I immediately felt so *light.* I also noticed that I immediately and significantly slowed down—just overall. It is as if my heart slowed, my thoughts slowed, my movement slowed. I simply was not in a hurry for anything.

I was able to savor the moment because I had no concern with what I "needed to do," which had almost always been something related to acquiring money, or *needing* money to do something. It is amazing how money has an impact on so much in our lives in ways we never even think of regularly. When you can completely let go of any attachment to the need for money—when you can *be* that you truly have unlimited resources and that money is simply not any kind of issue in your life—you suddenly realize just how much in your life money touches! It is a lot . . . and that is why so many people have such challenges around it.

In addition to the "slowing" of my overall pace, I also had a very marked psychological *and* physiological shift. I thought differently about so much. In the particular instance I am relating to you now, I was preparing dinner. I remember thinking, "We eat what we want, and have fun preparing it. This meal costs a lot of money and it does not matter at all because we can easily afford anything we want at any time." (Of course, I had that thought in a nanosecond, which went on for several seconds.) It was just such an intensely freeing experience. It was so powerful! I realized the concept of *being* wealthy on a whole new level, and I could literally feel my Energy shift.

It far transcended affirmations like, "I have all the money I need for anything I want." It was completely experiential and felt tremendously real, although as I mentioned, at first, I could only sustain the feeling for a few seconds. However, I believe those few seconds were a turbo-boost in the delivery of that reality.

Putting into words exactly what I do to achieve that state is somewhat challenging, but I think the first logical step is to state the affirmation in your mind. After that, you have to "step into it." I cannot think of another way to put it. You just temporarily "forget" that anything other than that the essence of your affirmation *is* the truth. Rather than focusing on "creating something new," simply forget about what you do not want to exist.

For example:

If your desire is to experience great wealth, but your predominant thoughts are on this "wealth" you *do not have*—even if you are trying to imagine yourself wealthy—you still have the whole, "I do not yet have this" conversation running. Even though you are not necessarily conscious of it, the "I do not have it" vibration is a powerful attractive Energy—attracting more of the same for you. However, if you can, even temporarily, *forget* that you do not have the wealth you want, then your "wealthy" state sort of becomes the de facto state for you.

I know this is a tricky one. I wrestle with the language here, as I am trying to describe something that is completely intangible and is much more linked to *feeling* than is possible to describe with words. It is about how strongly you can play with having your desire . . . and maybe the technique of forgetting might help you to experience that sense of play on a different level.

I can just tell you that I had been working a long time with "being" wealthy by doing the wealthy things like shopping for homes and cars. However, it was an entirely different feeling to approach these things with the true *feeling* that I had plenty of money (or means) to get whatever I wanted. Knowing *how* I was going to afford what I wanted was not the issue at all, on any level, not because I was thinking "The Universe *will* provide," but because I had taken it one step further and was actually feeling that "*the Universe has already provided.*"

So if you want to be a millionaire or someone who does not have to give money a second thought, be sure you play with the *feelings* associated with being that. Do not think and try to feel "a million dollars." Think and feel how it will be to have *no concern with money whatsoever* and hold that feeling as long as possible, as often as possible. That million-dollar level of wealth could come with a lot less or a lot more than a million dollars. Allow the Universe to deliver in alignment with what you truly desire, not what you think you *should* desire.

The Naysayers

In an earlier section, I discussed how people in our lives can be an obstacle in our journey down this new exciting path we're forging. I want to expand on one specific way this may occur.

It may happen that you have started integrating the scientific principles of the Law of Attraction, or at least you are trying to, but your spouse, friends or co-workers do not share your enthusiasm for this way of thinking. The big question I get is, "Will this affect the outcome of my efforts to manifest wealth?"

The answer is that it totally depends on you. Now, before I really get into that, let's back up and really look at your situation.

Remember that this spouse, these friends, these co-workers, or whomever it is that surround you and talk all of this down, are people that *you attracted into your life.* You first have to take responsibility for that. If you fight that basic truth, you are not likely to have success with these principles, because understanding that you attract everything, pleasant or unpleasant, is the distinction that gives you the confidence to create anything you desire.

You cannot just say, "I attracted this great thing, but this other situation is someone else's fault entirely." Remember, that does not mean that you *created* the situation. You have simply attracted it into your life, either through conscious, persistent thoughts or unconscious thoughts and beliefs that run without you even taking much notice of them. This combination of thoughts and resulting emotions creates your vibration, which then attracts appropriately.

When these people came into your life, you were most likely vibrating something very different than what you are starting to vibrate now. When you suddenly change "who you are" or work on changing your vibration to a new state, you are *going* to shake things up a bit among your sphere of influence. How can you not?

You also have to remember that the path you are on is *your* path. It is not our role to coerce others into our way of thinking or believing. In fact, if we do that when others are not ready, we are only going to create conflict, which creates negative emotion, all of which simply begins to attract more of the same!

What makes this harder is that the people who are giving us a hard time are often coming from the mainstream view of what is "responsible." So we hear things like, "Yeah, well that all sounds great, but the bills need to be paid now, and we have no money." If that sounds familiar to you, what is your first response when you hear this argument? Probably things along the lines of:

- They are right. This is goofy. What they are saying is perfectly logical.
- They do not know what they're missing. They are wrong. If they would just see it my way, we could change everything.
- They are making this so hard!

All of these are natural thought processes to have given what we have been brought up to believe, but entertaining these thoughts from others is sure to do nothing but lower your vibrations and attract more of their version of reality than the one you are creating.

So what do you do? Is their Energy affecting the outcome of what you are trying to create?

If you allow their thoughts to dominate your emotions, then they absolutely will have an impact. You also have to remember that these naysayers are not "wrong," per se, and certainly not in their own minds. Their belief systems are firmly entrenched and if they hear something they interpret to be "pie in the sky," they are not simply going to flip-flop into a new belief system because it sounds good. Actually, the fact that it sounds so good, or too good to be true, is likely to repel them.

What if you gave them absolute freedom to feel however they want about this and in no way attach their thoughts to your own emotions? After all, it is *you* who is being "unreasonable" here by society's definition. You are changing the rules of who you are and what you believe is possible in midstream. You have got to give the rest of the world time to catch up and a *reason* to join you, if that is what you want them to do.

You see, if you are challenged, be it by a spouse or friend, you have three choices:

1. You can bend to their emotional responses and slow or give up completely

on your journey into attracting the life you desire.

2. You can choose to no longer associate yourself with them if you find yourself unable to pursue who you truly are with them in your life. I acknowledge that this is a pretty harsh step, and I more highly recommend the *next* choice.

3. Commit yourself to creating a vision for *your* future. If you want your spouse, friends, or co-workers to be a part of that vision, then put them there. Focus on the feelings associated with having those you care about take this incredible journey with you.

Do not focus on *changing* them because that is not your job.

The third choice is a "lead by example" choice. Your only responsibility is to implement these principles into your own life wherever you can, and let those you care about watch what happens.

This more subtle approach will allow you to enter into conversation about what you are doing much more lightly.

In the meantime, just keep the peace. Do not try to rationalize with someone who is in a panic about money that the Universe will provide if they just raise their vibrations. That probably will not have the impact you are looking for.

Using the Law of Attraction to attain wealth does not mean to throw away responsibility. After all, if you do things you feel in your heart are irresponsible in the name of "proving your faith in the system," eventually your intellect will get the best of you. At a core level, you do not really feel good about being irresponsible. Plus, irresponsible behavior makes it even more difficult to get those around us to accept these principles as valid.

So again, lead by example . . . and do it quietly and peacefully. Eventually, if it is meant to be, those close to you will follow. If it is clear that they will only continue to work to impede your personal growth through negativity, doubt, and fear, then you have to make some serious choices or restructure your vision to include more harmonious relationships with these people.

Attraction versus Creation

There is a difference between *attracting* reality and *creating* it. While, at a quantum level, there really isn't any difference, I think that at a human intellectual level, there is a way of looking at attracting and creating so that you can more easily accept that you have these abilities.

By now, you should be very clear that *we are Energy* vibrating at a certain frequency. Our reality is a direct result of what we are vibrating. Our thoughts generate emotion that causes our vibration to shift, and we attract according to vibrational resonance. We literally magnetize our desires into our lives. But are we actually creating them from thin air, or is something else going on?

On one level, I have to say we *are* creating them from thin air. Nothing really exists in our reality without us observing it. This is a basic truth of quantum physics. Some people just have a hard time grasping that or knowing what to do with it exactly. Still, if we can gain an acceptance that we attract our desires through some kind of logical scientific process, we can move more rapidly through the work.

People look at their circumstances and think, "Did I create this? Did I create this house? Did I create hunger in the world? Did I create this woman (or man) I married? How could I create *everything*? How could I create high-definition television when I know nothing about electronics? Obviously, somebody else is doing something!"

Yes. We are all out here, creating and attracting our own realities. We are vibrating certain thoughts out into the Universe, some of them way below the conscious level, and as a result of our vibrations, we are attracting various things into our experience. The Energy that we are attracting and then "assembling" into our construct of reality could have originated anywhere in this vast ocean of Energy that is the Universe. We will meet, or come into contact with, other people or situations that are sending out a vibration that our vibration attracts.

So you are brought to a particularly unpleasant person by some means or you hear something on the news that sounds terrible, something you would never create on purpose. This happens because it is attracted to whatever you are vibrating. That does not mean that you *created* that bad thing. It simply means that whatever it is that you were vibrating to at that moment allowed that news to enter your life in some way.

It is not as though you consciously created a horrible train derailment or any other disaster. However, some combination of Energy did and, for whatever reason, your vibration attracted that experience into your life at a level deeper than you are conscious of.

You may have had the experience of thinking of someone and then suddenly having them call you one the phone. Maybe you thought of something you needed, an item like a pair of scissors or something, and suddenly they were in front of you. You can rationalize why they were there. It is not as though to your conscious mind they were not there, and then you suddenly materialized them. But that actually *is* what you did at a quantum level.

Why can you make things like scissors manifest nearly instantly (sometimes) and other things that you are really putting your attention on, like a new house, car, or relationship, seem to take forever? Well, the details are going to be different for everyone, but it always comes down to your level of resistance.

If we perceive something as big, we tend to immediately think of it as harder to attract into our experience. This belief creates resistance and makes that thought a reality. At the same time, if we really *needed* that pair of scissors we mentioned earlier, and we were fraught with worry about not finding them, all of our emotional focus would be on the fact that we couldn't find them and we'd spend hours searching without success. It has nothing to do with the physical size or monetary cost of something that makes it "big" to us. It's how we're relating to it emotionally that matters.

I want to share one distinction with you in hopes that it will give you another way to look at how all of this works and more clarity about the distinction between what we are creating directly and what we have attracted by accident. Those "accidental manifestations" are those things that have no apparent logic as to why they are there. Still, you must understand that it is *perfect* that they are there.

You should be thankful beyond belief that they *are* there—they exist for you because you have the incredible ability to design your life with your thoughts. All you have to do is work on cleaning up those thoughts—do it *on purpose* and take control—and you can design the life of your most passionate and exciting dreams!

Are You Feeling Stuck?

Sometimes when you start using these principles to create wealth, you experience frustration because things are not moving along the way you would like. I have heard from people who say, "I have been working with these principles for weeks now, and things just aren't happening. In fact, they seem worse now than before."

If the latter is true, you can be sure of one thing: Something *is* happening. You have started to become an active participant in your life. You have started *designing* your life, and the Universe is responding. Sometimes what occurs is not what you would expect or *want* at the moment, but the infinite intelligence of the Universe has decided that whatever is occurring for you is the most efficient way to deliver on what you are really putting out there.

Consider carefully the following things that can absolutely slow you down as you begin to consciously attract wealth into your life. Be honest with yourself here.

Are you crystal-clear on your vision? I know a lot of people read through material like this and keep all the work in their heads. They read that they are to write out their ideal day on paper, but they just never get around to it or they think that keeping it in their head is enough. Perhaps it is, but that can also slow you down. Writing brings your desire to another level of reality and helps you to solidify what you really want. This brings us to the next point:

Are you asking for what you really want, or are you asking for the means for getting what you want?

Are you asking for the house on the lake or are you asking for the *money* to buy the house on the lake? Money is a means to an end, but it's not what you should be asking for at all. Further, if you're struggling with wealth, it's clear that you already have resistance around money. Trying to attract money right off the bat without doing the necessary releasing of resistance around it (any negative thoughts or beliefs) is going to be an exercise in great frustration.

Now, you might find that money comes to you as a result of asking for that house on the lake (or more accurately, the emotions that you associate with having that house), or you might get that house by an unexpected means, but if you do not ask for what you *really* want, you are only delaying receiving it.

There is another level to this. Perhaps you ask for what you want, and then start looking for it to manifest in a specific way. For example, you ask for the nice new car, but then you do nothing but buy lottery tickets, expecting that this is *the* way you will get it. Or, you start looking for an increase in your business as *the* way you are going to get the *money* to get the car. So you are putting all your focus on something three steps away from your actual desire. You *must* stop doing that.

Are you having fun? Or have you made "creating your wealth" using these principles into a *job*? It is *not* a job and it should not *feel* like one. You are completely defeating the purpose of your journey if it feels like work.

Approaching your journey with the attitude that it is a chore does nothing but create a vibration that resonates "hard work" and wraps the whole process up in a layer of "yuck." The Universe does not try to figure out what you "really mean." The Law of Attraction simply works to attract more feeling of "yuck" or the feeling that this is a lot of hard work.

Are you putting a timetable on your manifestation? Of course you want your desires to be fulfilled immediately, but for most of us, our belief system does not support this. When you want something *now* and yet you actively do not believe it will happen *now,* it doesn't. Even if you have the idea that it *should* happen now, you do not believe it will happen now, so it never comes . . . because *now* is all there really is. Take a minute to let that absorb if you need to.

Do not worry about the timetable. Seriously. Your Ego demands results now, but impatience really causes you nothing but trouble and will keep you exactly where you are now. The Ego wants to stay in control.

Things will come to you at the perfect time, to the extent that you allow them to.

You have to remember that you are living a very human experience right now and depending on your background, this process of allowing yourself to have whatever you want can be fairly challenging. Your body—this physical experience—is just one small fraction of who you really are. You are an integral part of all source Energy, which has no inherit limitations whatsoever. This annoying little thought process called the Ego is keeping you small and limited, but only because you allow it to. Simply decide not to allow it any longer.

And of course the biggest culprit for feeling stuck is a lack of action. You absolutely *must* act in concert with the Universe once you put Energy into motion with your intention. It is only through action that you can have the experience of your desire fulfilled.

Creating With a Clean Slate

Another area of slowdown you may experience occurs from one of the first steps in the process of getting clear on your vision: deciding what you do *not* want and then using that as a springboard to getting clarity about what you *do* want.

Often we will identify a situation that we clearly do not want and make the decision that we want a different version of it, instead of something else entirely. You know you do not want something like a job or a relationship, so you say to yourself, "Well, I'd like this job or relationship to be this way instead."

Now think about what you have done. You are requesting that something outside of you that already exists *change* to your liking. What if it does not want to be changed? If you are in a relationship and it is not going the way you want it to, you might say, "Well, I want him or her to be *this* way in the relationship." Well, guess what? You cannot vibrate for them! You cannot change them.

However, you can attract something totally new and totally fulfilling. And before I go on to how you do that, remember this: if you are trying to change something, you will, by default, have some amount of Energy on what is "wrong" with it, adding more Energy to what you are trying to change or eliminate.

We are often much better served by beginning with a clean slate.

Close your eyes and just pretend you are starting completely over with your reality. You have a totally blank palette onto which you can paint anything you want. Of course, you are free to paint those things in your life that you already have that bring you great joy, but there is absolutely no necessity to include *any* version of the things that do *not* bring you joy.

In some cases that might not be too easy—especially if some of the "things" in your life that do not bring you joy involve people with whom you have shared a long history but who no longer support the vision you have for yourself. However, your attachment to *anything* out of a sense of guilt, responsibility, or whatever your Ego says you "should" feel about something, does not serve you or the person or situation in question.

For example, let's say you start this process in the way I am going to suggest in just a minute. Pretend you have nothing and know no one, just for the purposes of this exercise, and that you are about to create everything and everyone that you wish to be a part of your experience!

Start with your eyes closed, looking at this clean slate—Infinite Possibility. Now start creating your reality from the ground up. Where do you want to be? I am not talking about your house. I am talking about your geographic location.

The country? The city? Surrounded by mountains? On that lake we keep talking about? Create that picture.

What is the temperature? Cool? Warm? Is there a breeze? Feel it and smell it.

Now start to create your home. If you do not know where to start, gently ask the question: "What would my perfect home be like?" Trust me; a part of you knows exactly what that would be. Just allow any feelings or images to come in. Pay particular attention to the feelings and think about the essence of what you would like your home to give to you.

Freedom? Security? Peace? Let the feelings guide the creation of your images. Begin to add furniture, accessories—whatever you want.

Then you might create your prosperity level. How wealthy do you want to be? And more importantly, what would that level of wealth *feel* like? Does it feel in alignment with who you want to be in the world? Does it feel good? (Remember to use release techniques if you start feeling negative emotions around something you feel strongly that you truly do want!)

After you have had some fun creating your home and living environment, you can add the relationships you would like to have. There is really no specific order to all of this. I am just giving you an example of the process to give you an idea.

I want you to see the big picture here. *In this exercise you can have whatever you want.* That does not simply mean that you can have "reasonable versions" of either what you already have or what you can "figure out" how to get.

It means that *whatever you can imagine can be yours,* but you have to give yourself the freedom to paint that picture exactly how you want it, rather than how you think *others* would feel you should paint it.

One of the best ways to do that is to put yourself in the place—even for a few minutes at a time—where there *is* nothing else other than that which you are creating. You are starting completely from scratch.

Again, you can certainly choose things from your current reality to remain there, but do not use them as a starting point from which to "modify" your reality. Add them in, one at a time, only as you are sure that their presence in your reality will provide you with boundless joy and the freedom to be who you are and do exactly what you want to do to express yourself fully in your life experience! That is what this life is all about.

Meditation is a perfect time to do this. Tapping into source Energy and intelligence through meditation and creating that clean slate is a wonderful way to begin to attract what you *really* want. Of course, you want to be very much in touch with the *reasons* you want these things—and how they will make you feel. You will want to experience those feelings as fully as possible.

The basic idea here is to limit yourself in no way whatsoever. We are an integral part of an infinite Universe, filled with infinite possibility. Limitation is an illusion. Don't buy into it.

Intuitions and "Signs" of Delivery

When you begin to practice these techniques of attracting your reality, financial or otherwise, you are going to be looking for (and hopefully following) intuitive nudges and that appear to lead you in the right direction.

People or things will suddenly show up in your life for no logical reason. You might start hearing about certain job offers, or similar things that are fairly obvious to those even paying peripheral attention.

But if those are the only types of signs you are looking for, you are probably missing out on numerous opportunities to accelerate the realization of your desire. One of the places you should probably look the hardest is an area where you are sure something is not a sign. If you ever hear yourself thinking "coincidence," start thinking "sign" instead.

Also, sometimes we seem to get "signs" that things are going the opposite of the way that we want, but consider that the event that you think is so terrible—that you think is the opposite of what you want—is also very likely to be a sign. It also might be an awakening that perhaps you did not create a "big picture" in terms of your desire.

Here's an example. Let's assume that one of your strong desires is moving out of your current house and into that house on the lake. The house on the lake is obviously a symbol of prosperity for you—and yet you suddenly start taking financial hit after hit. You suddenly do not have money to pay your bills. All the while, you are desperately thinking "house on the lake, house on the lake," and the situation seems to accelerate in the wrong direction.

Finally you find that you cannot pay your mortgage and you lose the house you are living in. This is something of an extreme example, but what happened there?

Well, you *fulfilled* the first part of your desire to be out of the house you were currently in. Given your belief system, this might have been the most "efficient" way for the Universe to get you out of the house. Perhaps you never would have ended up in a house on the lake if you hadn't been "forced" to make a change. There could be a lot of reasons for that. You might have an inner belief that while you like dreaming about the house on the lake, you are really comfortable where you are and it would take a lot for you to actually take on a home of significantly bigger size and financial obligation. So to facilitate the desire that you just kept affirming to yourself, the Universe took whatever action would facilitate you first getting out of the current house.

Of course, it could have played out an infinite number of ways, but that is going to depend on your level of resistance to letting things flow effortlessly. What sequence of events would your current belief system allow to be unfolded in front of you? You can start to see just how important it is to really understand this stuff on a deep level. Ironic, because what we are really working so hard to do is simply return to our true nature. That is how far we have strayed from the our natural path of effortlessly living lives of passion and purpose. But the path is right there in front of us, should we choose to follow it.

I suggest that when you formulate your visions that you add the statement "for the good of all concerned" . . . and "I have all this or even better" and really *feel* the truth in it. Feelings in alignment with those statements create a vibration that allows the Universe some flexibility because you're not attempting to direct the universal laws in the process of delivery. If you see that the fulfillment of your desire is not happening or that something very undesirable is going on, go back and really look at how you have put your desire together in your imagination. Are there some built-in "implications," some "givens" hidden deep in your mind that differ from how you would write down your desire? Those are all attracting, too.

You might think, "Man, that Universe is a picky son of a gun!" But it really isn't. It is the most perfect reality-creation fulfillment mechanism that could possibly exist. *It gives you more of exactly what you put into it.* You just have to get extremely clear on what you are putting in.

So when it comes to "signs" and how to look for them, just know that they are everywhere and that they sometimes seem small and insignificant.

Look at everything, but do not obsess over it. Enjoy what pops up for you and follow your intuition all along the way.

As you get better at all this, it will not be such constant "work" to keep your head on straight. Your belief systems will shift and it will become natural. When you think you see a sign and you do not know what to do about it, just be still and ask yourself, "What do I *want* to do about it?" Then act upon that answer.

Ideas Are Energy and You Have Them for a Reason

While this concept may seem a bit more esoteric than some of the others, if you're starting to get a sense of the energetic nature of the Universe, you'll understand that's it's not really so "out there."

Did you ever have the experience of seeing a movie for which you had a very similar or even exact idea?

Did you ever think of an invention, and then a year or so later, that exact invention came out, created by someone else?

Perhaps a book you "wrote" in your mind but never put on paper suddenly appeared in the bookstores?

Now that you know a little more about Energy and the Law of Attraction, you can see that one of two things is possible:

1. You *could* have originated the idea, fully developed it in your mind (thus making it even more real) and then never took action on it . . . but the idea had been created. You did not just erase it—so the Energy of the idea was just floating around out there. Eventually, someone else might have worked themselves into vibrational resonance with that Energy and literally attracted your idea into their consciousness! They then took action on the idea and facilitated its coming into the physical.

2. Maybe it happened the other way around. Someone else originated the idea, did nothing with it, and it found its way to *you*, in search of some means to come into the physical. You *thought* it was "your idea," but it was out there already. You just *experienced* that it was your idea. Either way, you attracted it! Have you ever just had an idea pop in your brain out of nowhere, with no logical thought process even leading up to it? It was just there. Now you can see how that might happen!

So now that you know this, what do you do with it?

You first must realize that your inspired ideas are opportunities for you to fulfill your desires. They come to you at the perfect time and will hang around for the perfect duration for you to take action on them to fulfill your desires. If you do not act within that timeframe, the idea may very well move on to someone else as they become in resonance with it. You will always have this "residual memory" of this idea you had but never acted on, so when you see someone *else* fulfill your idea, you think, "Hey, that was *my* idea!"

So what is the lesson? If you have an idea, act on it, or understand that you are intentionally passing up an opportunity for your ultimate desires to be fulfilled. That is assuming, of course, that you have created a vision to live into, a desire that you actually are working on.

If you *are not* working on a desire, then the ideas you have will simply keep you in the reality that you are currently *unconsciously* creating. That is another reason to dream big and intentionally for the things you desire in your life. Do so because you are creating the perpetuation of whatever you are thinking about the most, whether consciously or unconsciously.

Remember that ideas are Energy. Depending on how long and hard you focus on an idea, its Energy is going to become all the stronger. The idea is destined for manifestation! You have the option of being its conduit into the physical. The Universe has determined that this is one of the more efficient ways for you to realize your goal. You can opt to take advantage of the opportunity or let your Ego give you a thousand reasons why you cannot or should not take action on it. There is not anything good or bad about either option. It is entirely your choice to create whatever you want, when you want!

Is every little stray thought a road sign from the Universe? Probably not (although it is an indication of what you're vibrating). I think you understand the types of thoughts I am talking about. The ones that seem inspired . . . or the ones that really get you excited . . . the ones about which you spend the most time thinking.

These are the ideas with the power.

By the way, it does not mean that you have to figure out everything about how to act on that idea. Just claim it and "be" that it has already happened. Feel that you have already facilitated the manifestation of that idea into the physical, and then allow the *Universe* to figure out the details regarding delivery.

You do not have to figure out where the money is coming from to build any prototypes. You do not have to worry about how Steven Spielberg is going to see your script. *You do not have to worry about anything. Be* that it has already happened and the Universe will lay the path out in front of you.

Do not complicate things by trying to intellectualize the whole process from beginning to end. Frankly, the Universe is going to provide a much better plan than we could probably ever figure out ourselves.

I know it is hard to give up that control, even when you want to. Your Ego totally freaks out when you try to do something like that! But just practice doing it. If you find it hard to totally give up control over the manifestation process, then just *pretend* you do not have a problem with giving up that control. It's a simple little trick, but you will be amazed at how effective it is.

So if you have an idea, no matter what it is, and it really lights you up, do not just stop at thinking about the idea all the time. Add Energy to it by thinking that you have already seen this idea through to completion and that it is a wild success. Then do not worry about how things will happen. Just start taking action as ideas occur to you.

Again, the ideas *will* come to you. You do not have to force them, which will, in fact, keep them from coming or make them difficult to recognize.

If you start this process, and then seem suddenly *bombarded* with ideas that begin to propagate into others more quickly than you could possibly take action on, simply choose the one that seems most appealing to you and take action on it. Be totally okay with putting the other ideas on hold or letting them go completely.

You see, you could say to the Universe, "I desire *this,*" whatever it is, and then suddenly the Universe could bombard you with a vast array of possible ways to do that thing. Just choose one of those ways, and the Universe will keep giving you the nudges that will help you continue that particular path (remembering, of course, that sometimes you'll be nudged in a completely different direction.)

You are going to have your desire fulfilled.

You are simply choosing the path to get there. There aren't any "wrong" choices. *All* choices will get you there in the most efficient manner possible—based on the choices you make along the way.

In the Face of All the Evidence

One of the most frequently asked questions I receive is also the toughest one to answer. It's not tough because there is any "trick" to the answer, but because the answer is often so hard to hear and implement. It goes something like this:

"I know we are supposed to think about how we are wealthy, but how can I do that when all around me I have reminders that I am not? I have got more bills than money and it is really hard to feel wealthy right now."

When people ask me that, I feel like they are hoping I will say something that I have never said before, like there is some secret that I have not yet divulged or some "shortcut" to the already very simple Law of Attraction principles.

Well, there is not. It does not get any simpler than this: get into the emotion of feeling wealthy.

I know that's much easier said than done.

You have spent your *whole life* integrating beliefs and feelings that have attracted your current situation. If you have evidence of "lack" all around you, it is because for years, you have been playing somebody else's game. You have bought into the mass mentality of "there is never enough," and as a result, this type of thinking has become a belief—a predominant feeling that attracts the circumstances that substantiate that belief.

So now this book tells you it is simply time to attract something else. You start chanting affirmations like, "I am wealth. I am abundance. I am joy." But as you are repeating this mantra over and over, you are staring at a stack of bills that you feel you can't pay.

If this is so, you're just wasting your time. Though you are "saying words," your *feelings* and *emotions* are vibrating something totally different. It is just like using any other affirmation that you do not really believe.

In fact, if your true attention is on your lack, you have probably also got a layer of conversation saying, "All this 'feeling wealthy' stuff is not working. I have been trying, and nothing is working. This is ridiculous. When is it going to happen?"

When you find yourself saying this, it is time to step up and take responsibility. It is not that the Law of Attraction isn't working. You are slowing it down.

You must understand that you cannot *break* the Law of Attraction. If you are not attracting what you want, it is absolutely because your predominant vibration is attracting something else. Plain and simple.

What do we do about that?

Consider that you were not born with a lack mentality. It is something that was taught to you over the formative years of your life. Your environment, which supported that belief, was the result of the predominant feelings of *others* who came before you. So if you were not exposed to anything different, how could you have possibly cultivated a belief in infinite and unlimited abundance?

As you bought into these belief systems, surrounded by *other people's* evidence as you grew up, you basically *synchronized* with their vibrations and made them your own. You became your very own magnet to lack, and you have been that way ever since.

How long does it take to change this? Ultimately, it is up to you. I know that everyone says that the *Universe* decides when and where a desire will manifest, but that will still always be in direct response to what you are vibrating. The Universe will deliver appropriately in accordance to what you are magnetizing, and thus allowing.

Here's an example.

Suppose you are thirty thousand dollars in debt.

First, you not only have to accept responsibility for the fact that you attracted that debt, but it would also help you greatly to be outrageously grateful for it, because that debt is the exact appropriate response to what you have been vibrating all this time. It shows you that the Universe does, in fact, respond perfectly! Knowing this, you now have the freedom of choice to vibrate something totally different!

Remember, you have been *feeling* this debt into existence on many levels, probably for many years. Just simply chanting an affirmation about being "wealthy" without any real *feelings* that resonate with those words will result in something that the Universe hears . . . something like this:

"I am wealthy . . . I am wealthy . . . I easily pay my bills . . ."

While at the same time hearing:

"Thirty thousand dollars in debt . . . thirty thousand dollars in debt . . . thirty thousand dollars in debt . . . How am I ever going to pay it?"

You have got two conversations running, and chances are very good that the *second* conversation about the debt has much stronger emotions connected to it, because it is your experience right now.

So what happens? You attract more stress, more fear, more worry, and possibly even more debt, because that is what you are truly resonating.

You see, it is not that the Law of Attraction is not working for you. It most definitely is working, just not in the way that you consciously want it to.

So what do you do?

Obviously, using a release technique is key here. All of these negative thoughts and emotions that come up for you are just resistance showing itself again. Release, release, release!

This is a great time to use the Experiential Meditation described in chapter 5. I get more positive feedback on this meditation than just about any other part of the "Wealth Beyond Reason" program, and I highly recommend that you start making this meditation a daily practice. Simply put, *it makes you extremely magnetic* for the period of time that you are using it. The more you use it, the easier it will be for you get into the feeling of having what you want, rather than thinking about what you do not want. That feeling will build and build until eventually the vibrational scales tip the other way.

However, a couple of things have to be happening at the same time:

One, be aware when you go back into a state of worry or fear around your money. My suggestion is this: when you come out of the wonderful feeling of experiencing your desire, no matter how long it lasted, be sure to express your gratitude for your ability to feel that way! Also, express your gratitude for everything around you right now, knowing that it is through this wonderful, seemingly magical power of the Law of Attraction that it is a part of your experience. If you have any residual negative emotions or belief, use EFT or another release technique until you feel their intensity vanish or significantly decrease.

Also, keep in mind that you *have* begun to start the trend in another direction, and that although you might have only felt truly prosperous for a few moments, *you have set the magnetic forces in motion* that will bring you all of the circumstances through which you can experience more of that feeling, provided you *allow* it and do not crowd it out with a lot of intentional negative thinking.

In the meantime, though, what do you *do* about the debt, particularly if you do not have the money to pay it?

Well, what *can* you do? If you do not have the money, you do not have the money! Worrying about it will solve absolutely nothing. I know it seems natural and logical to worry about it, but that's only because "worrying" is what you have been taught. You have associated all sorts of terrible things with the inability to pay a bill and, as a result, you attract those negative things. That is just the way it is.

Pay what you are able to pay, feeling gratitude that you can do so, and with the knowledge that extreme abundance is just around the corner. Instead of spending your time worrying, which is a counterproductive expenditure of Energy, focus instead on creating a vision of prosperity for yourself that is rich with the feelings of doing exactly and only what you love doing. You can make no better investment.

When you are in a financial crisis, what you really need is creativity. Fear and worry kill that completely, so you must use every technique at your disposal to avoid basking in those feelings.

I know it is tough at first. So what? Does that mean you should quit? Look, you either *strongly* desire a change in your life or you are content to keep making excuses as to why the Law of Attraction does not work for you. Well, *you* are the one making that statement seem true. The only thing you need to do is to commit *however long it takes* to turning things around.

It takes practice. That does not mean just going through the motions or saying affirmations to yourself that "I am wealthy," because, most likely, those words by themselves have very little meaning or power for you. Find what you most passionately desire in life, generate the wondrous feelings associated with that, and make those your focus throughout the day. You must, and I mean you *must*, watch where you have your attention. That is what is attracting your circumstances, be they good or bad.

Please, choose to put your attention on happy thoughts, and do it often—the more you do, the easier the process will become. It *has* to, because that is how the Law of Attraction works. Every time.

The Law of Attraction, Science, and Religion

We're really fortunate to be living in a time when information about the Law of Attraction is making its way to the masses. The things that we are learning about quantum physics are helping to bring the principles out of strictly the so-called New Age and metaphysical circles and into the mainstream . . . but that's not to say that those delivering the message are not without opposition.

Even with the advancements in our understanding of the scientific aspects of the Law of Attraction, there is still not enough traditional research and study to satisfy those who absolutely won't believe something until there are stacks of double-blind studies and the like to support the ideas being communicated.

Of course, if everyone were like that, then there would be no scientific advancement at all. After all, it is theories, ideas, and even simply intuitive notions that drive the significant advances in science.

Throughout history, it has been the visionaries—oftentimes the people who were mocked and ridiculed, yet held their vision of what they've known to be true —who eventually created the word's most significant breakthroughs in science and advancement.

The popularity of *The Secret* really brought the naysayers out. The mainstream media took the message of *The Secret* and immediately tried to discredit it. This isn't true across the board, of course. In fact, *The Secret* being featured on *The Oprah Winfrey Show* twice in a week was a major contributing factor to the explosion of exposure the film and book are getting.

But alas, the more popular "good news" is the more it is resisted by those whose job it seems to be to resist it, the bigger it becomes. And you will of course see this pattern over history. Tell someone that their lives can be magical—even miraculous—and those bringing that news nearly always face the wrath of those who oppose such a notion. Luckily, most of today's messengers aren't facing the same fate as those a couple of thousand years ago.

It's hitting home for me personally, of course, because I *am* one of those messengers—and of course there are many more messengers of the Law of Attraction than just those of us in *The Secret*. We're just getting the attention right now, so you're seeing some of the teachers brought onto programs to "debate" the Law of Attraction. It's unlikely you'll ever see me in that position. For me, it's not debatable, and the people who want to debate it will have their lifetime of resistance and attracted evidence to support their positions. Further, in a media situation, a person generally has about thirty seconds to answer any one question, and often the interviewer gets the last word and gets to skew the conversation however they need to to support their position. I'm not faulting them for that. It's their job. My background is the media. I understand that they do what they do for their reason. I simply choose not to play that game.

I'm not an evangelist for the Law of Attraction. I'm not trying to twist anyone's arm to believe it. My role is to facilitate the learning, understanding, and implementation of these principles for those who are in resonance with them, or at least open to understanding them if they don't quite yet. This is what makes my work joyous. Anything else is just a job. Trying to sway someone's opinion takes too much work. That's not to say that a person won't change their opinion after listening to what we have to say—it's just that our attention isn't on changing someone who doesn't want to be changed. That's just misdirected Energy, and takes me out of the flow of what I truly love to do.

Because of the nature of what I do, I see more than enough evidence of the truth of the Law of Attraction. And yes, much of it is simply a knowing—a knowing that cannot be expressed 100 percent accurately with written or spoken words. It is an understanding that permeates every cell within me, and there are countless thousands—even millions who have the same knowing. I don't need a scientific journal to tell me that the Law of Attraction is at work in our lives any more than I need a scientific journal to tell me that oxygen keeps me alive. It would keep me alive whether or not I ever read a study on it.

The Law of Attraction is the same way. It's at work in the lives of every entity in the Universe. For that matter it's at work throughout everything in the Universe, whether it's "alive" or not. It's simply how Energy works. And whether you believe it or not, it's going to keep behaving the same way.

Of course, as I always say, by its very nature, if you don't believe in the Law of Attraction, you will attract all the evidence you need to support that position—and of course the irony of that is that it's the

Law of Attraction that brings you that evidence. But some people will never see that . . . because they don't *want* to see it . . . and they will never be in vibrational resonance with seeing it, so they will literally resist any proof that is contrary to their position.

This is why it's highly unlikely that we're going to see, at least any time soon, any scientific studies on the Law of Attraction that are totally conclusive and satisfying to everyone. There are studies that prove that the outcome of experiments are often affected by those doing the observing. There is a book called *The Holographic Universe* by Michael Talbot that you might want to look at for all sorts of interesting studies along these lines.

Because the Law of Attraction responds to an individual's vibration, you could take two scientists, give them the exact same set of test conditions in a Law of Attraction experiment, and they can attract completely different outcomes based on what *they* bring to the experiment vibrationally. If one *knows* the Law of Attraction to be the truth, and if they have no (or very little) resistance in the key areas that are likely to be affected by such resistance in a test condition, they will attract quite different results than a person who has a tremendous amount of resistance to these ideas . . . because they can each only allow into their experience those things with which they are in vibrational resonance.

In my mind—and keep in mind that I'm a very analytical and "prove it to me" type of person—I've seen and experienced more than enough evidence. And all of us in the world who share that knowledge are admittedly on a leading edge of all of this. That is to say, we're ahead of science, so to speak. Perhaps the day will come when, just as the reality of the Earth being round finally was able to be proven scientifically (though it was just a "crazy thought" for quite some time), science will find a way to prove the Law of Attraction enough to satisfy virtually everyone.

Although that will be a great day and a major accomplishment, there is no need to wait for that day to put these principles to use.

Now, the other challenge that Law of Attraction teachers are facing (should they so choose to face it), is that there are large numbers of people who have somehow made this a religious issue—or more accurately, they believe that the Law of Attraction and the teaching of it somehow negates or opposes their theological viewpoints, whatever they may be.

And I hate to put it so bluntly, but these people simply aren't listening to what's being said. They are taking the message that we can live our lives by design and construe that to mean that we are taking God, or whomever they put their religious faith in, out of the equation—when precisely the opposite is true.

It *is* true that in the Wealth Beyond Reason program, we don't use the term "God"—and that is out of respect for those who don't resonate with religion, or who use different terminology to refer to whatever force created this Universe. But this does not in any way mean that learning about and embracing the Law of Attraction as a real force in our lives dishonors this creator. What better way to honor the creator than to use the gifts that we have been given to the fullest extent possible? To use a somewhat silly example, it would be like my giving my son a set of building blocks and then observing him not using them to create anything because he felt like it was *my* job to do all the creating—when in fact I *want* him to use the blocks to express himself creatively, which is why I gave them to him in the first place. Okay, I said it was a silly example, but hopefully you get the point.

But to speak to those who do have a problem with this message because they think we're bypassing God or not giving credit where credit is due, I want to say this. All of this is only possible *because* of the creative force that put all this into place. It is the utmost honoring of this force to be who we are, and to use what we have been given. Perhaps all people don't do this honoring the same way, but to be who we are and to follow our natural sense of purpose and passion is, in my opinion, the most powerful honoring one can do.

We as Law of Attraction teachers are simply teaching about one very powerful law that the creator of this Universe, whoever or whatever that is, has put into place. Further, it is a law that allows us to fully experience our existence as human beings to its fullest potential, and do you not think that is the intention of the source of this creation? Why else would we have desires, imagination, and dreams, if not to pursue and eventually realize them?

And it is through the infinite intelligence of this creator that all of this becomes possible. There is not one thing that most Law of Attraction teachers teach, myself included, that goes against most traditional theological teachings. There are always what I would call extremists in virtually any theology, and again, they're simply not going to hear what I'm saying and stick with their beliefs, and that's fine. I'm not trying to change anyone's faith, because I think of what we're doing as completely independent of any religious faith whatsoever. It's as if we were explaining gravity . . . another law put into place by the creative force, which we needn't fully understand or believe in to have it be an inescapable part of our experience. Law of Attraction is, at least in this time in our history, a much different kind of law because it *does* open up a tremendous amount of personal power in our lives where before we may not have seen it, and of course there are many reasons why over the years we've been cut off from this knowledge—which is why the movie was called *The Secret* in the first place. It's not that we're teaching something that no one has ever known . . . but the fact is, the vast majority of people do NOT know how the Law of Attraction is working in their lives.

So we're at a very interesting time in our history. The word is getting out, and people are either embracing it, considering it, or outright rejecting it. This is the way of things. My hope is that it will resonate with as many people as possible so that we can all begin realizing that we are put here to explore our passions, contribute our greatest value to the Universe around us, thus furthering our collective advancement as human beings—because we've been given great gifts and unbounded potential in a truly abundant Universe—and now, finally, the understanding of how to make all of this a reality in our lives.

If it's not a message that resonates with you, or if you have a level of resistance to that level of freedom, then I sincerely invite you to be okay with that for yourself, but I also ask you to consider the true value of ridiculing, mocking, or naysaying something that is so clearly having such a positive impact on the world—even if it's not *your* version of the world that it's impacting.

Prayer and the Law of Attraction

How does prayer fit into the Law of Attraction?

My personal definition of prayer is an "intentional communication or communion with God"—and that's whatever you consider God to be. You can call it Source, the Universe, or other terminology with which you're comfortable.

I call it an "intentional" communion, because in reality, we're always communicating with the Universe. We're a part of it. We can't separate ourselves from it, and there's no way to "conceal" our vibration. Our vibration is whatever it is we're putting out there. That means that whatever we're thinking or feeling is creating the vibration that we're emitting, the Universe is always responding to that, and there's nothing we can do to prevent that.

So we're always communicating. We're always, in essence, asking for something, even if we're not doing it intentionally. We are literally "asking" for what we want every moment of every day, because we're always putting out a vibration to which the Universe is responding.

Prayer, on the other hand, is a practice of intentionally putting out a specific vibration . . . and of course, this can take many forms. We could bow our heads, clasp our hands, cross our legs, and meditate—whatever action we call "praying." We direct our thoughts and feelings toward a specific end. It could be asking for something. It could be expressing gratitude.

You have to realize, however, that there is nothing more magical about prayer than there is in any other moment in our day. It's not the like God or the Universe ignores everything else we're vibrating unless we preface it with the thought, "Okay, I'm praying now."

However, *you* might significantly shift your vibration when you get into the action of praying. You may become more focused. You may create a feeling of reverence or something similar which will change what your predominant vibration looks like to the Universe—and thus you will shift what it is that you're attracting.

Because of this, prayer can be a most powerful state, and it can either be of great service to you or disservice to you, depending on what state you are in when you pray.

If you pray in a state of desperation—"Oh, God—my financial situation is so terrible. You've GOT to help me or I'm doomed."—then the Universe will, as *always,* respond to your vibration, and you are likely to attract more of what is perpetuating your desperate financial state.

The power of prayer is well-documented, and even the slightest bit of research can demonstrate that apparent miracles can occur as a result of prayer. However, the Universe will deliver these miracles appropriate to the vibration that is being sent as a result of these prayers.

For example, if you are praying for someone who is sick (who by the way, has the desire to be well . . .) then your prayer should not be, "Oh God, please deliver John from this devastating illness . . . we can't bear to lose him" or things along those lines. Instead, the vibration that is in alignment with healing is more like, "Thank you God for the health and vibrant Energy that is permeating John at this moment. We delight in his well-being and we are grateful for it."

This is a vibration that attracts health, whereas the first "prayer" only focuses Energy on the disease.

What I'm hoping that you'll understand is that in reality, you're always in a state of prayer—even if it's not intentional. But when you do intentionally enter into prayer, it's important to be aware of what you're putting out there, because it can be even more powerfully attractive simply because you are being intentional and focused with the words you're using as you formulate your prayer.

So by all means, if you are a praying person, know that prayers are heard and responded to by Universal intelligence at all times, but they will still be responded to in accordance with the laws put into place by the creator, and your understanding of these laws will allow you to pray in a most powerful and productive way.

Tithing and Giving

One of the most controversial topics that are discussed with regards to the Law of Attraction is the topic of tithing. This is because there are many teachers who stress tithing as a way to ensure abundance. This brings up many questions.

Where should one tithe? Do you have to? What happens if you don't? Why only 10 percent? Why do some believe we should expect exactly a tenfold return on our tithe?

Much of what we know about tithing has simply been passed down throughout the years. Many different religions and spiritual organizations have touted the importance of giving 10 percent of our income to either help said organization further their spiritual work, or as payment to God, or any number of other things.

But how does tithing play into the Law of Attraction? Is there a direct connection?

First, let's just make a quick distinction between the concepts of "tithing" and simply giving.

Tithing is basically a gift of 10 percent of your income that you should give to the source of your spiritual growth. This is a more liberal definition than simply saying that you should give 10 percent to your church. What if your church doesn't contribute to your spiritual growth? That's not uncommon. What if you grow spiritually because of the work of some secular organization, or an author of a book, or a friend or associate? Wouldn't your tithe be more appropriately given to them?

Giving, however, is just that—*giving* . . . to anyone for any reason, simply because you want to. There are entire books written about a "law of tenfold return" and how you can expect such a return for anything you give, provided that you "claim" it.

So why is it that I receive email from people telling me that they tithe, or give, and yet they see no return?

There are all kinds of responses that I could give about being patient, or that the return doesn't always show up as money, and so on—and those are all true—but the real answer lies in only one thing, and always will: it fully depends on what those people are putting out in terms of an energetic vibration, thus allowing themselves to attract in the form of a return.

If a person tithes with a "well I doubt this will work, but let's give it a try" attitude, then are they in a state of allowance? No! They are basically challenging the Universe to "test" this idea of tithing. This type of vibration totally repels such a return.

The same holds true for giving in expectation of a tenfold return. While it's true that you can expect a return for everything you give, this is only true if your expectation is one of a kind of detached knowing, rather than a "well, where is it? I *expect* it!!" These are two totally different vibrations. One allows, one repels.

There have been those that teach that if you don't tithe, the Universe will take it's 10 percent anyway.

This taking could be in the form of things like needing unexpected repairs to your car, or having someone get sick and needing medical bills paid, etc. There was definitely a tone of "bad things will happen to you if you don't tithe."

Now, is this true?

Well, because of the simplicity of the Law of Attraction, the answer is both yes and no. I have come to the conclusion that it is not an "across the board" fact that things will be taken from you if you don't tithe.

Here's the bottom line in terms of scientifically looking at this issue:

You absolutely cannot experience anything that you do not allow through your vibrational allowance. In other words, if you believe and are in resonance with the idea that there will be some kind of retribution for not tithing, you can most definitely expect that there will be.

However, the Law of Attraction only responds to your vibration. How you give is much more important than what percentage and all of that.

Ideally, you're giving from a place of abundance. Because the Law of Attraction demands that you attract according to you vibration, then if you are in a place of "I have more than enough to give joyously to whomever I want," then you will attract the situations and circumstances that make it possible for you to give even more.

Still, we serve ourselves through our giving when we do it joyfully and freely . . . not because we're trying to get the Universe to pay us back, but because we know it will . . . and this isn't an intellectual "yeah, I get the concept" type of knowing—I mean we know it as fully as we know we're going to take our next breath. This is the vibration we want to achieve. It's when we know that there is truly nothing but abundance, and giving of ourselves takes absolutely nothing away from us, and in fact attracts more.

Tithing and giving, while they are differentiated by definition—one being a giving to your source of spiritual growth, and one just giving to give—they are both governed by the Law of Attraction in terms of how our giving "attracts."

So my bottom line on tithing is do it with joy and gratitude for those whom you are tithing, and your rewards can be great—more than tenfold, if you allow it. If you believe in karma (that what you put out comes back to you) then it would make sense support the source of your spiritual fulfillment, but I don't think that there is a Universal Law in place that says that you'll be punished in any way if you don't—except to the extent that you believe you will . . . and that's when the Law of Attraction plays a role.

The same is true for simply giving. Some people absolutely love to give, and many times the giving is its own reward—and other times, they actually do see a tangible return either monetarily, or in some other form, because they are attracting and allowing that return to come. They aren't trying to force it. They aren't waiting with their arms crossed, tapping their foot thinking, "Okay, where is it?"

So give! Give like crazy! But be very clear what your vibration is when you're giving. Give with detachment to any specific outcome. Give with a knowing that the Universe is Infinite and Abundant and ready to flood your life with prosperity! When you give with this feeling, you are sending a very clear signal to the Universe that you know that the supply is infinite, and that by giving, you are merely acting as a channel for this abundance, and that there is much more where that came from. This is the magnet you want turned on in your life, and this is the magnet that will bring you everything you can possibly imagine.

When Things Seem to Fall Apart

Another very common question that comes up with many people just starting to work with these principles is why things seem to go in the opposite direction of how you want them, particularly when you first start working intentionally with the Law of Attraction.

The first thing I want you to notice is that things *do* change when you start shifting your intention. For the moment, don't worry that things don't seem to be changing the way you want them to—just notice that you are, in fact, having an impact on your experience of reality . . . and despite how you're interpreting what's unfolding, I hope that you can actually get a little excited—because it's a clear indication that these principles are real—that we do actually have some conscious control over how our reality plays out.

But why do things seem to be going in the opposite direction? If we're doing all the "techniques," if we're clear on our vision and we're visualizing, then *why* do things sometimes seem to crumble around us?

There are several reasons why this can occur, so I want to address a few of them. Do any of these pertain to you?

First, very often people make the mistake of interpreting what occurs as they begin this work as bad or negative—because that's how they've learned to interpret these events their entire life. A very common example is when a person is focusing on a different career for themselves and suddenly they lose their current job. It's automatic for a lot of people to immediately panic—and it's totally understandable. Their old way of thinking immediately interprets the situation and creates beliefs about it—such as the idea that there will be no income, or that bills won't get paid, and all those other natural, "Oh no, I lost my job" reactions.

However, it's just as simple (but not necessarily easy) to interpret the job loss as an opportunity. I know that's a lot easier said than done when you're actually in the situation, but that doesn't change the fact that the Universe is always responding to your vibration. The choice you make on how to feel about any experience is going to determine how things unfold for you from that point on.

What really should happen in that case is that you continue to do whatever positive visualizing you were doing to put you in the state of feeling that you truly want, and pay close attention to your intuitive nudges for the next action to take. If you do that without resistance, you'll be appropriately led to what you want, even if you can't figure out how that's going to happen.

But again, it's natural for us to try to "figure out" what to do next—how to solve this "problem" . . . but in most cases, this line of thinking will not serve your higher vision. Many times people panic and just try to get whatever job they can, and put their dreams on hold until a "better time." That's not to say that finding some kind of temporary income replacement is a bad idea provided your intention is still to take powerful inspired action toward your vision and to not stop taking that action until you step into that vision.

And the job loss scenario is just one example of how people immediately tend to react to a situation in what you might call a socially appropriate way . . . to panic, to worry, to feel fear or sadness or other similar feelings. These are all learned responses, but they are not required, and in fact will keep you stuck, or worse, create a downward spiral that really leaves you wondering what you did to make the Universe so upset with you.

But remember that the Universe doesn't get upset with you. It's simply responding to your vibration. If you panic, you'll attract more about which to panic. If you see infinite opportunity—or more appropriately—if you *feel* infinite opportunity, then that's what will come to you—but you'll need to be on the lookout for it so you can take action.

Another reason things sometimes seem to go "backward" is simply resistance. If you've been coasting along with a negative or kind of flat-lined outlook toward your life, then suddenly shift gears and try to create a more positive scenario, then resistance really shows up powerfully—screaming at you the alleged "truth" of the absurdity of your new vision. "It's too big. You don't deserve that. *How* will you do that?"

And the more powerfully you visualize the positive, the more powerfully the resistance shows up—and because those negative feelings are the ones you're most used to having, it's much easier to be in resonance with those—and because they've now been amplified because of the contrast of the feeling you're trying to generate with your visualizations or other techniques, you more powerfully attract situations that are in resonance with those negative feelings.

Unless you recognize that and do something about that resistance, it's no wonder you're left feeling like this whole Law of Attraction conversation is some kind of cruel joke—when in actuality, it's working perfectly—just as it always does. But *you* have to recognize, take responsibility for, and change the way you're honestly feeling in a given moment.

Many people try to mask what they're really feeling if it's negative with a lot of positive talk—because they believe it's wrong to have a negative thought. But masking your true feelings with positive talk or affirmations isn't really going to change your vibration, at least not in a timely manner. You actually have to get in there and do something about that Energy that is not in vibrational alignment with what you want. In other words, don't lie to yourself. Own your feelings—negative or not. Don't judge yourself for having them, after all it's to be expected for most people to experience negative emotions from time to time.

Once you own those feelings you're free then to imagine a life free of those feelings . . . with a knowledge of the truth that all beliefs and feelings can be changed to better suit you desire yourself to be, but that it's going to take some action. And by action, of course, I'm referring to releasing—either via EFT, The Sedona Method, or any other technique out there.

Although I sound like a broken record, you've got to release resistance if you want to make progress, and you have to be brutally honest with yourself about the feelings that you're experiencing. Trying to deny having feelings that aren't in resonance with what you want will not serve you. You've got to deal with them, or you'll just keep getting the same results you've always had, or as we're talking about here, they might actually be amplified because you're consciously trying to attract something else—by *feeling* something that you're not used to, creating a great sense of contrast. Just remember that panicking in what you perceive to be a desperate situation, while understandable, does not let you out of the Universal process of attraction.

This is why I say the Law of attraction is not a toy—but a powerful force at work in our Universe that *will* respond to your thoughts and feelings, which create your vibration to which the Universe is responding.

Finally, another reason things seem to fall apart is that people are so busy doing the exercises and techniques that they're either not "hearing" or they're not responding to the intuitive nudges that they do get. They're waiting for something that makes logical sense to them. They want a some kind of sign that seems to line up with the end result they have in mind. And that's simply not how it always works.

You have to own that your familiar ways of thinking and reasoning have gotten you into the situation that you're not trying to change. Using that same reasoning will not allow you to change. You have to go "beyond reason" . . . see with bigger eyes, if you will. When the ideas come to you that seem to fly in the face of everything you consider to be logical, then those are the ideas you're most likely supposed to be acting upon to accelerate your progress.

But too often, people don't pay attention to those ideas . . . ideas that they've actually attracted by doing whatever techniques they're doing . . . and since they don't act on them, nothing happens, and yet they wonder why this Law of Attraction thing isn't working. It's not the Law of Attraction that isn't working.

Working successfully with the Law of Attraction is not about passively waiting for things to appear out of thin air, even though it can occur that way sometimes—and when it does, it's simply an indication that there is very little resistance in that particular area. This is about working in concert with the Universe. You ask, you receive, you ask, you receive—always. But what you receive isn't always immediately going to be your end result. You're going to receive the next logical event in the process of this manifestation. Sometimes it will be an idea, sometimes a chance meeting, or some event that takes place that when acted upon will bring you to the next step in the realization of your vision. But you have to take those steps as they come, or obviously nothing is going to change, and you will wonder about the whole process.

When you're just getting started (or if you've stepped away from this work for a while), it can seem like slow going. It does indeed take practice to hear and trust the intuitive nudges. But commit to practicing this, which you can only do by releasing resistance on an ongoing basis, and taking inspired action. That's all you have to do. Don't spend so much time interpreting events as either good or bad. Just notice them, keep your vibration in resonance with the end result, and enjoy the journey.

Unimaginable Optimism

We are fortunate to live in a time where the understanding that we can actually live our lives by design is becoming more widespread. While certainly not everyone embraces this idea yet, there are more people considering this as a possibility than ever before! Of course we also have more people arguing against these ideas than ever before as well simply because more people are hearing about these ideas which are so contrary to the generations of limitation-based thinking we've cultivated.

This seems to be the normal cycle throughout the ages. New ideas that go against traditional thinking come to the forefront, and there is vigorous opposition until finally a preponderance of evidence sways even the most skeptical of naysayers . . . or at least enough of them to change the predominant belief on the planet in a way that makes a significant difference.

Admittedly, we're very early in this cycle but provided that those of us who do have an understanding of all of this put what we know into practice and pass this knowledge down to future generations not simply by teaching principles per se, but by leading by example, we have the opportunity to shape the future of the world in a very powerful way.

At the risk of sounding like a kind of Utopian visionary, I do believe that if the idea of living a passion- and purpose-filled life were instilled in children from the time they were born, we'd be well on our way to creating a planet where all the pieces of the puzzle fit together perfectly; a world where everyone would be sharing their natural gifts and reaping abundance naturally without the need to negatively impact the life experience of others. I acknowledge that there is a lot that needs to happen before anything close to that is likely to be a reality—but it all starts with you, living a life of passion and inspiring others to do the same.

The greatest thing we can do now to ensure a long rich future for the planet is to nurture the passion in our children instead of squelching it. Often we derail our children early in their development unintentionally because of the limitations we've learned and the idea of what is practical. In other words, we act and speak in our children's best interest, but is what we say really going to result in them feeling confident about living the lives they truly wish to live?

The best way to cultivate a paradigm of unlimited potential in our children is to be a living example of it. Teaching, as I say, is not enough. We must show them how to work in concert with the Universe by getting clear on our own passions, creating a life based on those passions, and allowing abundance of all kinds to become a part of our experience. If we cannot demonstrate this to our children, then all the knowledge we impart on them about these principles is impotent.

Wherever you are in the progress of your life, it is never too late to start changing your experience of reality for the better. Depending on where you are in your journey, you have many significant levels of resistance to deal with before you start experiencing dramatic change, but now you are armed with the tools to do just that.

A belief that "it's too late for me, but I'll try to teach my kids, my friends, or family" is simply not going to work. If you want to help create future generations of deliberate creators, you must first become one yourself.

Accept your magnificence. Embrace the miracle that you are. Acknowledge that although you may have gotten off track here and there, that you are a powerfully creative being put here on this planet to fully engage in the experience of life. It is significant that you are here. You have been gifted with all of your unique abilities and desires so that you may experience them.

Go for it!

Recommended Resources

While there is a lot of information available on the Law of Attraction and related activities, the recent flood of resources to choose from can also be part of the problem we're having of effectively transferring this information in a usable way.

Because there are suddenly so many "experts" in the field, it is difficult for the average person to discern who has information that will actually be usable, practical, and effective.

I've created this section to point you to information that I know is not only good, but truly outstanding with regards to effectiveness. Some of these resources I mention in the text of this book, and others I invite you to explore on your own.

Boundless Living

www.boundlessliving.com

This is the online home to programs from Bob Doyle. Here you will find the Wealth Beyond

Reason program, our online curriculum in the Law of Attraction. Additionally, Boundless Living offers an exclusive membership area that provides access to all of Boundless Living's program, DVDs, and educational events, plus an online community that provides support and accountability.

The Experiential Meditation

www.wealthbeyondreason.com/freemeditation.html

We have made a free download available of the Experiential Meditation described in this book. The meditation is fully produced with music and voice guidance, and can be downloaded in the MP3 format suitable for play on your portable audio player, or for burning onto an audio CD.

Carol Look, Master EFT Practitioner

www.boundlessliving.com/carollook

Bob Doyle and Carol Look have worked together many times. Carol possesses the outstanding ability to guide people through the process of meridian tapping to bring about profound changes. With specialized programs in abundance, weight loss, eyesight, and more, Carol's programs are highly recommended to expand your ability to release resistance in a profound way.

The Sedona Method

www.wealthbeyondreason.com/sedona.html

In this book, the creator of the Sedona Method, Hale Dwoskin, discusses what the process is all about. You can access an audio interview with Hale at the web address above and actually be walked through the process.

The Healing Codes

www.boundlessliving.com/healingcodes

Dr. Alex Loyd has created an amazing system of healing at the level of cellular memory. Aside from the obvious benefits of improving one's health so that they can more fully enjoy the results of creating an inspiring vision, the Healing Codes technique is also a highly effective resistance-releasing tool and deserves your investigation.

Vision Board System

www.boundlessliving.com/visionboard

In this text, I mention that I used something of a "digital" vision board to start experiencing results with manifesting "stuff" like cars, exercise equipment, and even a change in my banking account. Since that time software has been developed to make that process even easier, and the "Vision Board system" is a complete software solution that allows you to create multimedia vision boards that you can view on your computer.

Mind Stereo

www.boundlessliving.com/mindstereo

I'm a big believer and fan of what's known as brainwave synchronization technology. This allows you to fine-tune your brainwave state using nothing more than specially encoded audio. Traditionally, stereo headphones are required to experience the intended effects, but that has changed.

Mind Stereo is a piece of software that allows you to create your OWN brainwave synchronization audio from any piece of audio you'd like. This means you can create your own meditation CDs with your favorite music, or even music that you stream from the Internet in real time! The program comes with many interesting presets, and you can create your own custom programs easily as well.

The Passion Test

www.boundlessliving.com/passiontest

Janet Attwood's Passion Test has proven time and time again to help reconnect people with their sense of passion when nothing else would. The test is only a few questions long, and I highly recommend that you take it if you feel at all stuck regarding what your passions are in life.

About the Author

Bob Doyle is the CEO of Boundless Living, Inc., a personal development company based in Atlanta, Georgia that teaches people practical methods to live their lives by design. His Wealth Beyond Reason program is an online curriculum in the Law of Attraction, which takes a mainstream approach to a subject often lumped into the New Age category.

The effectiveness of Bob's teaching gained the attention of the producer of *The Secret*, and subsequently he was one of the featured teachers in that film. He also created the Boundless Living Challenge, which has facilitated powerful transformation in the lives of thousands of people in the area of their passions and previously elusive dreams by providing an online community of support and accountability, as well as a wide variety of tools and other resources to help people stay in inspired action.

A champion for creative self-expression, Bob is also a composer, writer, and photographer. Visit him online at:

www.wealthbeyondreason.com

or

www.boundlessliving.com.